Parenting Toddlers

A Step by Step Beginners Guide for Better Child Development

(Simple Steps to Great Baby Sleep)

Mark Carpenter

Published by Rob Miles

© **Mark Carpenter**

All Rights Reserved

Parenting Toddlers: A Step by Step Beginners Guide for Better Child Development (Simple Steps to Great Baby Sleep)

ISBN 9781990084317

All rights reserved. No part of this guide may be reproduced in any form without permission in writing from the publisher except in the case of brief quotations embodied in critical articles or reviews.

Legal & Disclaimer

The information contained in this book is not designed to replace or take the place of any form of medicine or professional medical advice. The information in this book has been provided for educational and entertainment purposes only.

The information contained in this book has been compiled from sources deemed reliable, and it is accurate to the best of the Author's knowledge; however, the Author cannot guarantee its accuracy and validity and cannot be held liable for any errors or omissions. Changes are periodically made to this book. You must consult your doctor or get professional medical advice before using any of the suggested remedies, techniques, or information in this book.

Upon using the information contained in this book, you agree to hold harmless the Author from and against any damages, costs, and expenses, including any legal fees potentially resulting from the application of any of the information provided by this guide. This disclaimer applies to any damages or injury caused by the use and application, whether directly or indirectly, of any advice or information presented, whether for breach of contract, tort, negligence, personal injury, criminal intent, or under any other cause of action.

You agree to accept all risks of using the information presented inside this book. You need to consult a professional medical practitioner in order to ensure you are both able and healthy enough to participate in this program.

Table of Contents

INTRODUCTION 1

CHAPTER 1: WHY SELF ESTEEM MATTERS 8

CHAPTER 2: THE JOY OF RVING 12

CHAPTER 2 17

CHAPTER 2: WITH PRIVILEGE COMES RESPONSIBILITY 24

CHAPTER 5: RAISING A LITTLE GIRL: THE BASICS 34

CHAPTER 6: PUSHING LIMITS 37

CHAPTER 7: HOW TO RAISE HAPPY CHILDREN OF DIFFERENT AGES 48

CHAPTER 8: THE WOUNDED INNER CHILD 54

CHAPTER 9: WHAT DO YOU UNDERSTAND BY SENSORY SIGNALS 57

CHAPTER 10: THE 24/7 JOB 60

CHAPTER 11: UNDERSTANDING YOUR CHILD 63

CHAPTER 12: COOKING 71

CHAPTER 13: CHILD DEVELOPMENT PHASES 81

CHAPTER 14: CHILDREN WITHOUT RULES BECOME FRUSTRATED ADULTS 89

CHAPTER 15: THE BEAUTY OF PARENTING 99

CHAPTER 16: HELPING YOUR CHILDREN TO SOCIALIZE .. 103

CHAPTER 17: SINGLE DAD WITH TODDLERS: HANDLING TEMPER TANTRUMS 108

CHAPTER 18: HOW TO BE A DAD 116

CHAPTER 19: WHAT'S WITH 'NO!'? 135

CHAPTER 20: BRAIN AND EMOTIONAL DEVELOPMENT OF CHILDREN. AND HOW CAN YOU USE IT. 143

CHAPTER 21: UNDERSTANDING CHILDISH TANTRUMS .. 152

CHAPTER 22: CHALLENGE 5 – EMPLOYMENT ADJUSTMENTS 165

CHAPTER 23: HOW TO BE A BETTER STEP PARENT 171

CONCLUSION 177

Introduction

It would not be surprised to anyone that around the world these days, that in every family, there is some elements of Long Distance Parenting in existence. This parenting technique is as a matter of fact, practiced by parents knowingly or unknowingly due to the shift in the paradigm of the global economy.

Certainly, circumstances such as, going to work in order to earn a living will force parents to leave behind their kids to be cared by someone else. Also, people travel on official or business trip out of town and even traveling abroad in search of greener pasture. All these and many others would lead to parenting the children from a distant location.

Additionally, whenever there is a divorce in any marriage, the affected parents would resort to long distance parenting in order to prevent the absence of any of the parents affecting the rearing of their kids. The cordial relationships between the parents and the children should be of paramount importance to both parents in order to maintain a loving parenting environment.

Imagine a situation where in a father, mother or whoever is in-charge of parenting the children comes home and they fail to acknowledge his or her welcome due to absent from home without communicating with them. The children need parental care, love, and concern in their social, emotional, psychological and spiritual orientation during their evolutionary periods of their lives.

As parents, we should start performing our divine duty of parenting from wherever we happened to be at any given time. We should not leave completely the rearing of our children in the hands of people who may not be truly bothered whenever things go wrong. The modern technologies of the current century have made, "Long Distance Parenting," very doable and less stressful. Parents should therefore take good advantage of the gadgets around today and follow the developments going on in their children squarely.

Certainly, in this book, parents will not only become aware of how to deal with the difficulties involved in long distance parenting but also learn the best and acceptable methods in parenting children in this modern time. From time immemorial, parents' good and cordial relationships with their children are the most essential things any good parent should hope to achieve in this lifetime.

This practical and simple handbook titled, "Long Distance Parenting," is loaded with rich tips that will give an overview of some of the difficulties involved in rearing kids. It also has offered some suggestions that can be applied by parents' daily routine of parenting of the children.

Quite obviously, a lot have changed in the world because of the Internet existence and nowhere is that more prominent than in this book. In the past, it was difficult for parents who left their children behind and had gone to work or lived elsewhere to inquiring about the welfare of the children they left behind from the caregivers.

All that have completely changed, one can call from almost any part of the globe within minutes. It was extremely difficult to place a phone call to your home from the office or anywhere in abroad due to complicated protocols in the telecommunication systems in the past, especially in third-world countries. But now, all that have changed for the better. So, parents have no excuse anymore not to ask about the welfare of the children whenever they are not physically present.

Now, due to technological innovations, the Internet and many other possibilities have made parenting from faraway remote locations very stress free. Parents can call their homes from the office or anywhere in the world to inquire on the situation of things at home and about their children well-beings. Therefore, parents who are not always at home physically in parenting or rearing their children, can stay away from home and still perform their duties as parents towards their kids with ease. Well, all thanks to the modern day technology.

Practically, long distance parenting is practiced by so many parents in our world today, even though some parents don't know that they already engaging in it somehow. As a former public school teacher for more than 10 years before I decided to travel abroad in search of greener pasture, my children were more or less being looked after by other people at home. I used to wake up very early in the morning to go to school and only to return in the night and most of the time, the kids would be fast asleep. It was really very difficult to practice long distance parenting those days. But with the improvement in the information technology, I started applying the principles of long distance parenting in rearing my children without even knowing it.

Candidly, when I lived abroad without my children, I was making use of the technologies available today in parenting them from afar. Imagine, my youngest child, who was only 2 years old and the youngest of my 3 children, is now in grade school. I was physically absent in parenting them but could have coped due to my frequent communication. I communicated with them almost on daily bases and with the people who are physically around them.

As long distance parenting is what a lot of parents do daily, I think reading this informative document would always be quite handy and helpful to parents out there. I am quite certain that parents would benefit from reading through the pages of this book. They would be able to know which methods or techniques in child parenting would be more suitable for them in order to relate effectively with their children. That would enable their children grow up to be well-rounded kids who can contribute to the general advancement of our societies and live honest, fruitful lives rich with glory and integrity the way they are naturally meant to be. Take a look at "Long Distance Parenting" now. I know you'll like what you see.

Chapter 1: Why Self Esteem Matters

Did you know that 85% of the world's population suffers from low self-esteem? This is according to Dr. Joe Rubino as shared in The Self-Esteem Book. Did you also know that 90% of all women around the world desire to change at least one part of their body? Among girls on 5th to 12th grade, 59% are unhappy with their body shape while 81% of 10 year old girls are afraid of becoming fat.

Girls who want to lose weigh because of what the media feeds them are becoming alarmingly numerous. The age when girls are exposed to negative "teen" issues such as sex, dating and vices are now happening at earlier ages. In fact, about 73% of girls ages 8 to 12 are now acting, talking and dressing like teens.

By ages 12 to 15, self-esteem may hit rock bottom because of puberty entering the picture. This may lead to feelings of depression, suicidal tendencies, rebellion and a host of problems that every parent can prevent if you nurture self-esteem early on.

What is Self-Esteem?

In a world where people are quick to judge and the pressure of looking good is at an all time high, self-esteem is one thing that can help your child weather the negativity.

Self-esteem is like self-worth which pretty much tells you how much a person values himself or herself. It is the measure of how much your daughter likes herself not just physically but also from the inside. If self-esteem is high, it can be her armor against a cruel world full of bad influences and toxic people.

As self-esteem is a collection of one's belief in oneself and experiences as well as what other people say, it can change from day to day, year after year. The pattern is developed over the years and it starts early on in life. According to one study, it reaches its peak at age nine, plummets at age 12 to 15 then revives at age 20.

Why Self Esteem is Important?

With all the upcoming changes that will come your daughter's way, self-esteem is very important because it is the anchor that will keep her feeling worthy about herself despite what people say and what's happening around her. But ultimately, it is important because it plays a major role on how healthy she will be mentally, emotionally and behaviorally through the years.

Low self-esteem leads to a domino of teen issues and problems while high self-esteem will steer your child to the right friends and hobbies. Because she feels good about herself, she will also feel more in control of her life including her strengths and weaknesses.

While self-esteem is never consistently high, it pays to build a strong foundation while early on in your daughter's development process. The middle years which starts from age 6 to 9 seems like the most ideal time to teach her about her worth and encourage her to explore her abilities and potential.

What's Your Role as Parent?

As parent of a young girl in her preteen years, ages 6 to 8 in particular, you have a golden opportunity in your hands. Like every parent who wants their children to be happy and successful, you need to take advantage of this period in your daughter's life when she is still more receptive to your guidance and advice.

At this point of development, it is important for parents to take an active role in teaching your child about self-esteem. Do not be a bystander like most parents tend to be and never wait until the tumultuous teen years to salvage her low self-esteem. If you want her to grow up confident and someone who knows her worth from the inside out, you need to take your job as mom and dad seriously.

Chapter 2: The Joy Of Rving

The joys of RVing come from all directions. We all like the idea of parking our RV near a beautiful, scenic area and we know the joy it can bring. Waking to the sound of waves slapping on a shore or a tinkling brook can get most travelers smiling. If you like to RV with friends, the sound of laughter around a campfire or the view of a wooded lot may make you happy. Once a baby arrives, it's not time to give up your love of vacationing, but rather a time to realize that an RV is the best way to travel with a family of young children.

People have loved vacationing in recreational vehicles for many, many years. However, often people think that once a baby is born, their RVing days are over. On the contrary, traveling with a baby can be a real nightmare without the convenience of an RV. Consider the following reasons to reinvent the way you see your recreational vehicle so that you can enjoy your family fully as you travel.

Home away from Home:

Many children get 'out of sorts' when they are away from home. There are a few, brave baby souls who embrace change and sleep anywhere you put them down. However, for most parents, this is not a reality. It can be hard to travel with a baby because as soon as you get them acclimated to one room, you're off to the next leg of the journey. This can leave both the parents and the baby exhausted and wishing for the vacation to end. If you have several children in the family, this phenomenon expands and it can lead some families to choose not to travel at all. When children become uncomfortable or over-tired during a trip, it affects everyone.

An RV can be a great way to get a child settled into a home-like routine. They can sleep in the same bed every night, stay on their schedule, and feel relaxed in their home away from home. It's very easy to bring items from home to make them feel comfortable. You can easily bring favorite blankets, pillows, and toys that might be too bulky to bring in a car or to drag in and out of hotel rooms. In fact, you don't necessarily have to kennel a pet that the child may be attached to. By bringing the family dog or cat along, it may sooth a child and makes them settle in more happily for a long, family trip.

Baby Items on Board:

Most RVs have creative storage solutions. This means that you can bring all of the baby items you need to make life comfortable. Instead of renting strollers, you can bring your tried and true stroller. A pack & play yard or folding fence could make the difference between a fun day and an exhausting day.

Safety Items Available:

You can be rest assured if you have the space to pack necessary safety items, medicine, and baby care products that will help you to feel relaxed knowing that you have everything you need to take care of anything from a bug bite to a fever. With your child safely contained in their car seat on the road, you will have peace of mind while enjoying the experience.

No Hotel Hassle:

Have you ever pulled into a hotel well past bedtime and tried to drag all of your luggage and baby items as well as the baby into an elevator to get to your room. Somewhere between the first and third floor, with the baby crying since he/she was wakened to come in to the hotel, you probably wished you hadn't tried to take the trip. With an RV, there are no problems like this. You have everything with you and your self-contained 'full suite' travels on wheels so that the RV can simply be parked; leaving you to nestle in and relax without carrying a crying baby down a hallway and rooms full of sleeping strangers.

Food, Glorious Food:

When traveling with babies and children, food can become a big issue. Eating out can become not only expensive, but troublesome. Traveling by RV gives you so much more control over your child's eating habits. If you have a young baby, you can easily prepare bottles or nurse in peace within your RV. If your child is already on solid food, you will have everything there and easy to access within your own space.

Older children can become cranky if their diets are altered too much. Also, it can ease some of the stress when families don't have to eat out for every meal of the day. This can cut down on many family arguments about where to eat.

The cost of eating out may not be an issue for your family. But consider how nice it would be to choose when to eat at a restaurant and when to stay in your cozy, little home on wheels.

Chapter 2

The first thing I want to cover is turning no into yes. This doesn't mean saying yes to everything a child wants, but rather presenting alternative solutions or even helping the child find alternative solutions on their own. This is perhaps better described like a compromise. Finding a way to solve the underlying problem without necessarily giving in to their desires.

This can be difficult at first, but like any habit, it takes a lot of practice to make work. In fact, the same could be said about any of the techniques presented in this book.

Studies have shown that the mind will cling onto negative words longer than it clings to positive words. There's a lot of talk about changing the way that we talk to ourselves, making the choice to enforce the use of positive terminology rather than including words like no or not in our self-talk. This is the same concept as turning a no into a yes. It's picking and choosing how things are worded to make it easier to find a different solution than just saying no.

So, how would a person turn no into yes without giving in to every demand? It's a delicate situation, to teach them to that there are other ways. The first step is to find out the reason behind the request, sometimes its easy to discern like if a child wants a piece of candy, they really want some kind of treat. Other times it's a little more difficult, as the frequent tantrums of an overtired child. If it's not easy to identify the cause of the request, that's when it's important to pay attention to what the child is saying and how they're saying it.

Young children do not communicate their feelings well, and preteens and teenagers often do not want to communicate much with parents. But parents know their children, even if you can't ask the kinds of probing questions that would tell you the true motivations. Keep in mind that sometimes a piece of candy is just a piece of candy, it really could be that simple. Try not to overcomplicate things, that will make this process more difficult if you try to read to deeply into it. Sometimes kids just want something that they know they're not supposed to have.

Again, practice will help with this. As you start to identify their motivations, they will learn this practice themselves. Some children even start to come to you with what the problem and speak about it, but if bad communications have already formed in the family then it may take a while.

Once the motivation is assessed, it's simply finding a way to solve the problem collaboratively. Often this is started by offering alternatives that still solve the problem instead of just saying no. "Would you like an apple instead?" It's a common thing that parents already do in several ways. Offering an alternative, but this can be taken even further, by asking the child how they can solve the problem. Finding out if they have ideas, normally this doesn't take much. I've found that children adore talking about their ideas on a regular basis for the most part, and if they were part of the solution it will improve their self-worth more than something just being given to them.

An example of this would be a child wanting to go to summer camp. The motivations are easy to assess. They want to be independent, learn things on their own, spreading their wings outside of the parental identity and camp is definitely a great thing, but money is tight and it may not be affordable. That's where the struggle comes in. You want to say yes, but you can't afford to tell them that you can do this. It's a bad feeling, but like anything else, maybe you can turn this into a learning opportunity.

There is a couple of different ways to handle this. For older children, I suggest talking to them honestly. Tell them the financial struggle to solve this problem, and communicate any other concern you might have. Ask them if they can think of any sort of solution to the issue. Often times the answer can surprise you. Maybe they can help earn the money to go. And suddenly a solution comes to light. Even younger children can help earn the money. The way my house solved the problem was to have the children go to friends and family and ask them all to save soda cans for them. It may not be enough, but there's also hitting public parks for soda cans that people throw away. There are tons of other ways that kids can earn money, babysitting or mowing lawns, helping friends and family clean up their houses and yards, carrying or chopping firewood. Dozens of ways to make just a few dollars at a time, giving them the opportunity to turn a no into a yes all on their own.

Not only does this give them what they wanted, but it encourages creativity and problem solving and encourage independence to solve their own problems. My own children now come to me with solutions on how they can get it themselves when it's something they want instead of just begging me to solve the problems for them. They have been empowered to find solutions and become a better person, thinking about what's reasonable and how much work it would take to get the things that they want. They learn worth and value and figure out their limits and lines on their own. It's a valuable lesson that follows parenting in a more positive light.

I'm in no way advocating letting children do something dangerous, there are still times that no is the only viable answer, and don't be afraid to tell them no if what they want is absolutely off the table, like having treats before dinner or riding in a car without a safety belt. These are times when the power of no should be used, but a lot of no's in everyday parenting can be turned into a yes with some creative thinking. I've personally found that the hard no's were easier to accept if my kids trusted me to work with them if there was a possible way to solve it without saying no. It increased the trust that if I had to say no, it was for a good reason, one that couldn't be solved easily any other way.

There are many, many ways to build the kind of trust that makes a family work well together, to build the kind of love that lasts a lifetime and doesn't end every family gathering with a fight, even if we do love watching those families in sitcoms it doesn't work well for living our day to day lives. Sitcoms are based on dysfunctional if loving families, but it's possible to be loving while cutting out a majority of the dysfunction and misunderstandings.

Chapter 2: With Privilege Comes Responsibility

Adults realize that with privileges come responsibility, but that is a lesson the parent has had many years to learn.

To teach your child this principle you may wish to use the following exercise. Give each child in the family a box or basket and tell them to pretend the house is on fire and they have 10 minutes to put their very favorite possessions into the box and return to the starting point. Explain that this is simply a game and is nothing to worry about.

Once everyone has returned to the living room, or wherever the discussion is to be held one or both of the parents takes out their driver's license and their bankcard.

In one hand, hold up your drivers license so everyone can see, and in the other hand, hold up your bankcard.

Ask your group whom they believe the cards belong to. Most will say they belong to the person whose name is on the card. (If you're lucky enough to have a kid who gets it right off ask him to stick around – tell him you may need his help before the game is over).

The point is that, even though the person whose name is on the card paid for the card, the cards really belong to the issuer - not the person issued the card.

To retain rights to the card the person whose name is on the card must follow rules, regulations, laws and terms of agreement or they could loose their card and all the rights associated with it.

Now, it's time for the parent to take back the authority that their child may have wrestled away from them.

The parent needs to explain that even though the things in the box belongs to the person holding it – the adult who paid for the items is the legal owner, and the person using them items has simply been issued the items under certain terms and conditions.

Tell your teen that just as the state or the bank could revoke your use of the card they issued to you, for failure to comply with their terms, the same thing can and will happen to them if they fail to comply with your terms.

Reassure them that as long as the rules are followed neither you nor they have to be concerned with loss of privileges.

As the parent, you may wish to set up a warning system whereby your teen is given up to 3 warnings before action is taken against their item, but they need to understand that you have issued their items in good faith, and that you expect them to respect the rules that are associated with continued use of the items.

Try to end this exercise with a pleasant experience such as cake and ice cream so everyone feels safe at that point.

Note to Parents:

Children really are people from conception. They have the genetic make up of individuals with their own likes, dislikes and temperaments.

Parents can and should try to teach basic life principles to their children, but sooner or later children are destined to make their own decisions – and the decisions they make are not always decisions the parent agrees with.

On the other hand, the decisions they make may not be disagreeable ones either.

Experience tells me that once children reach the adolescent stage of life parents are there basically to offer whatever support the child is willing to accept.

Parents often try to soften the blow for their children (I did this myself) and try to cushion the penalties their child will inevitably feel when their actions result in unpleasant consequences.

Some teens avoid chaos by observing the results of mistakes, bad choices or even rebellion their siblings or peers go through. Our two younger children were much easier to support through their teen and early adult years than was our older son.

Sons two and three were more mature and trust worthy as teenagers, and thus able to enjoy many more benefits of the resources we could offer as well.

The bottom line is this. Accept who your child is and what level of maturity they have reached. For example, if your teen is old enough to have a drivers license but is too immature to respect the people who provide for him, or cannot independently perform age appropriate duties and responsibilities; then you might want to hold up on giving him a 3000-pound car or truck to drive around town in.

Does this mean you will likely be inconvenienced? Yes. Understandably, a teen being able to drive him self is a tremendous asset to a parent, but a teen that is careless or irresponsible with an automobile is likely to bring more than inconvenience to their parents' doorstep.

Teens Need Parents who are in Control

The main point of this chapter is to advise parents to get control of them selves before trying to get control of their teenager.

If you are out of control you will never be able to be the parent your child needs you to be. If you need anger management classes then, by all means pick up the telephone and find a class. Get on the Internet and start researching and reading books on how to control your temper.

You may even need to seek professional help but don't just sit there doing the same thing you've always done. You cannot explode into a rage and expect your teen to remain calm. If you don't have an anger issue that needs to be dealt with then I can make a few suggestions that might help you when your child becomes argumentative.

First, something you may want to consider is the fact that your teen wants to communicate with you and will do so on whatever level you allow.

So, talk often to your teen about things that are non-threatening to them. Find pleasant things to discuss at length with your child.

Long, inconsequential discussions will let them know you enjoy interacting with them. It's called, "making conversation".

Have you ever known anyone who seemed to enjoy a good argument? For some people screaming matches can become addictive. There are chemicals that are released when people are threatened known as the fight or flight reaction.

Some people even get addicted to a feeling of excitement when natural epinephrine is released into their bloodstream.

The key to ending the argument before it ever starts is to say whatever you have to say, and simply shut up.

If "no" really is your answer – there's no need to speak another word. If you simply can't make yourself "shut up" then you need to remove yourself from your teen's airspace.

Go outside if you must, go visit a neighbor. Without explanation, simply say, "I'll be right back" and leave the premises.

It's extremely difficult to argue with someone who won't converse with you. Teenagers usually try to argue their point ad nauseam, or they'll try to make their parent explain the undesirable response they were given to their request.

Just be certain that "no" is your final answer, and then pretend you have lock jaw! (To add humor you could even point to your jaw).

Misguided, compassionate parents try to help their teen understand something that clearly, the teen is too immature or else unwilling to understand.

By pass the pleading, begging and possible explosion, and simply give your answer then abruptly end the discussion. Teenagers are smart. Before long your teen will know where the cut off point is.

Whenever you make a new rule be sure to explain to everyone affected, at a time when the rule has no bearing and in full detail the reason for the rule - then stick to it!

You can rest assured that someone will be inconvenienced by the rule, so be prepared to ride through a few rough waves until the rule is firmly established.

Use non-argumentative methods to enforce your rules whenever possible. For example, if your rule is no showers past 10pm then draw up 5 gallons of water at 10pm and turn the water off if you must.

Another approach would be to turn the hot water heater off at 8pm.

Chapter 5: Raising A Little Girl: The Basics

Raising a child, especially a girl, is not at all an easy task. Setting the foundation of character early on in your daughter's life will pave the way for you to raise a well-rounded, sweet and spirited girl.

Be a Role Model

The golden rule of parenting is to always show your children the kind of person you want them to be. Remember that children are impressionable. If you wish to have a well-mannered, kind and honest daughter, do your best to show these characteristics to her. Researchers point out that the negative influences that your daughter will see will only serve as a validation for the things that you end up teaching her at home.

Kindness

Another trait that you should teach a little girl early on is to be tolerant and open to the differences of people. Once your little girl understands this, she will be able to appreciate the works of others, and will also be able to work with them in a friendly way.

Balanced Parenting

Part of raising a well-rounded and sweet little girl is to make sure to strike a balance; you should be able to teach her independence and the value of following rules. She should understand early on that she can have a lot of fun but that she cannot do what she wants all the time. Most of all, remember that the best method of chastising a child is not through punitive, but corrective methods.

Be Supportive

Be supportive from the get-go. When your daughter is old enough to go to school and participate in sports or activities, remember to act as a parent and not as a coach. Remember that as a parent, you should be supportive. Do not be harsh or critical. It is the coach's job to criticize; let her do it. Your job is to keep your daughter's self-esteem intact and help her succeed in what she likes doing.

Do not limit her options

You may have a little girl but that does not mean that you should only expose her to girly things. Let her decide if she wants other things like ball games instead of ballet lessons.

These tips should come in handy when your daughter is younger, but things are likely to get more difficult when they get older and reach the adolescent stage.

Chapter 6: Pushing Limits

We give them all the love that we can, we cherish them, and then we find ourselves wondering why they must always push the limits that we set for them. It can be frustrating as a parent of a toddler when we don't really understand what they are going through. Often, we forget that they are very sensitive, extremely emotional and that they lack any impulse control whatsoever.

We tend to take it personally when our toddler pushes the limits, feeling as if we are failing as a parent or that the toddler does not love us. It is important for us as parents of a toddler to understand that these little people can be overwhelmed by the emotions that they are feeling and that even though they may not want to behave a certain way, they have no control over the impulses that they feel.

The most important thing that you can remember as the parent of a toddler is that the child does love you, and none of their behavior should be taken personally because it is not directed at you. The child appreciates everything you do even if they cannot express it, and he or she needs you to care for them more than you will ever know.

As the parent, you have to remind yourself that this type of behavior is normal, that it is healthy and that there is a reason your child is pushing the limits, even if you have to tell this to yourself a hundred times a day. You need to internalize this, ensuring that you are not blaming yourself or feeling as if you have failed your child.

The big question still remains; why do toddlers have to push limits? There are many different reasons why toddlers push limits, and one of these reasons is that they are hungry. Raising three children, one thing that I did learn was that a toddler seems not to know they are hungry until they have gotten to the point of "hangry." If you have ever been so hungry that you have gotten to the point of being angry or upset, you know what I am talking about.

A toddler seems to be able to push through hunger, not noticing that they need food, even when it is offered to them. However, when they get to the point that they must have food, they become overwhelmed and do not know how to express what is going on with their body.

This brings to mind the story of a young mother of a toddler that I know. She was having a barbecue with all of her friends, her toddler was usually very well behaved, however, it had been a long day, and it was hot outside. The toddler was playing quietly with a friend when, all of a sudden, he bit the friend. The mother gasped in horror as her child collapsed in tears and began throwing a fit. Suddenly she realized that she had been so caught up in talking to her friends that she had not stopped to think if her child was hungry. Quickly she picked him up, promised him food, but began talking once again.

The child wiggled in her arms, kicked, and began screaming. It was obvious that this mother was rarely seeing this type of behavior from the child, but she understood what the problem was. She had promised to feed him, but became preoccupied quickly and had forgotten just how hungry the child was.

Once the child had eaten, he was back to being his angelic self and played nicely with the other children.

This behavior was in no way the child's fault. He only knew that he was hungry, he was trying to get the attention of his mother, and he was willing to do it anyway he needed to. Once he had her attention and she promised him food, he calmed for a moment, but upon realizing that he had lost her attention again, he began pushing the limits once more struggling with her in order to get what he needed.

What we can learn from this story is that when your child starts pushing the limits, look for something that the child needs. This could mean that the child needs to be fed or even that the child needs to be put down for a nap. When the body needs something, it will take control of the child, and the child will display attention-seeking behaviors in order to get that need fulfilled. This is not the child misbehaving simply because he or she wants to misbehave.

Another reason that toddlers push limits is that they are seeking some clarity. Of course, your child knows that they are required to behave a certain way.However, they want to know if those rules still apply when you are tired or when there is company over. The child is going to try to push limits when they are put in a new situation simply because they want to know if those limits that are regularly put on them are going to apply to the new situation.

This is when you need to make sure that you are being consistent with your child. Of course, there are going to be times when your response to certain behaviors is going to vary, but no matter how you respond, you need to show the child that the rules never change, you are still the one that is in control and that their behavior is not a threat to you.

Many parents allow their children to run wild when they are away from home, let's say for example, at a family get together, simply because they do not want to leave the event. However, you have to be the parent; if the child is pushing the limits that you have set for them, trying to find out if the rules still apply, you need to make sure that the child understands that they do apply, and if they cannot abide by the rules, you will leave the event.

I see this happen all of the time at the grocery store. Make sure that your child knows you will leave the store, nothing will be bought, and you are not afraid to do so. It does not matter if you do not have enough food in your cabinets for the next week, you will find a different time to shop or do without. After a few trips back out to the car with nothing, your child will understand that the same rules that apply at home, apply at the store as well.

Children also push limits when they are trying to express their feelings. They feel emotions very strongly and have yet to learn how to control these emotions so many times, they come bursting forth like a flood taking us completely by surprise.

An example of this might be a child throwing themselves on the ground and crying because they do not want to leave the park. Now you have two choices when it comes to how you can react to this. You can get angry at the child for feeling their feelings, tell the child they are never going to the park again and stomp off in a rage. Or you can let the child know that you understand they are upset about leaving the park, you know he or she is disappointed but that it is time to leave.

This shows the child that they are not going to get a reaction out of you, which is another reason that children often push limits. We need to encourage our toddlers to feel the feelings that they feel and not be ashamed of them, but also show them that just because they feel a certain feeling, it does not mean the plans change.

When it comes to trying to get a reaction out of an adult, many toddlers push limits. This is often because the child is seeking some type of control over the adult, and it is often the effect of the child being in control most of the time. It is important for toddlers to know who the boss is. If they feel that they have control of the situation, most of the time, they are going to continue to fight for that control when you try to set limits.

If you find yourself in this situation currently, it is going to be a bit harder for you to set limits for your toddler. However, it is not impossible. What you will find is that the toddler is going to fight harder when you set these limits, trying to hold tight to the control that he or she has had over you in the past. However, when you stick to your plan, the toddler will quickly realize that you are the one in charge, not them.

Toddlers will also push limits because they need attention and, for many, it seems to be the only way that they can get the attention that they need nowadays. You see, there was a time when parents did not have their faces stuck in phones, tablets, and computers all day long. There was a time when they actually interacted with their children on a regular basis. If your child feels as if they are not getting the attention that they need, they will push limits, they will act out, and it is simply them, saying, "Hey, I'm still here, and I need you."

Make sure that you are putting the electronics away and spending time with your toddler every single day, getting down on his or her level and doing things that they enjoy. What you will find is that there are a lot less limit pushing and a lot more happy times together.

Finally, many toddlers push limits because they do not have a strong leader to follow. In other words, they are doing what they see you doing and when you are upset with them for doing so, they do not understand why.

If you want your toddler to be respectful, you yourself must be respectful of others. If you want your child to be kind, you must be kind as well. Imagine, having a leader that did not want you to behave the same way that they did, one that set your standards higher than they sat their own. How confusing would that be for us as adults? Imagine how much more confusing it has to be for a little toddler when they are put in the same situation.

Toddlers push limits for many reasons, some of it is part of who they are and some of it is learned behavior. If what you are dealing with is a learned behavior, the good news is that it can be unlearned by setting the right example for your child and being consistent with your expectations.

While it can be frustrating at times, it is important for us as parents to remember that limit pushing is often done by a toddler that is trying to learn about the world around them. It is up to us to teach them how far they are allowed to go and what limits cannot be crossed.

Chapter 7: How To Raise Happy Children Of Different Ages

Bringing up kids from childhood to being full-grown adults is a daunting task, which requires resilience, dedication and self-discipline. Giving advice on raising happy kids is not an easy task either, especially because children at different ages require different parenting skills. How your 7-year-old son uses his pocket money is probably not how your teenage daughter manages her savings. As such, there are different strategies to deal with toddlers, children between 6 to 12 years and teenagers.

How To Raise Happy Toddlers

Toddlers are probably the easiest children to read emotions from. When you come home from work, you notice a big smile on their face when they see you. If they can't find something, they sob uncontrollably. However, beneath it all, you have to wonder. Are they content? The signs are normally very conspicuous. A happy child is playful, smiles, shows curiosity, exhibits interest in other children, and is easy to stimulate. On the other hand, an unhappy child is usually withdrawn, does not eat much, is quiet, does not play, ask questions, laugh or smile, or get spontaneously interactive with other kids. It is however important to note that if your kid is naturally introverted or shy and does not interact or laugh a lot, it does not mean that they are unhappy; shyness and sadness are not the same. Consequently, you may require more effort to read the signs. If you notice major variations in their behavior like being more fearful and isolated, this might suggest that your child is facing problems that you should address.

You need to understand some signals that toddlers may use to express their feelings such as enjoyment and interest, which are positive feelings, and fear, anger, and distress, which are negative signals that contribute to an unhappy kid. An easily upset and fearful child is more or less an unhappy child. However, many parents fail to realize that an angry child is normally communicating sadness. Excessive distress, no matter the age, is what causes anger. When your 5 year old hits their sibling, or throws away their toys, this shows that they are distressed beyond their control. Your toddler may probably have their own way of expressing distress when they are going through a hard time. He or she might withdraw, throw tantrums, or become clingy.

As you learn more about your child's temper, you will get better at studying the signs when something is not right. In addition, find time to have fun with your toddler. In as much as they would enjoy chocolate for dinner and nonstop entertainment, what actually makes them happiest is basically just you; this is the first stage at raising a happy kid. Bond with them, and play with them; if you find it fun interacting with them, they definitely do too. Play is not only joyful, but is the basis for development of essential skills necessary for future happiness. Spontaneous play provides a forum for your kid to discover what they love to do; they want to come up with buildings using blocks, play doctor with their toys and so on, all of which can dictate their lifelong interests.

Moreover, help your kid learn and master new skills. People who have mastered a skill are usually happy. For instance, when you teach your toddler how to throw a ball, they learn from their mistakes, develop discipline and persistence, and then reap the joy of achievement through their efforts. In addition, they enjoy recognition from others for their achievement, and discover that somehow they have control over their life. This is especially important because the next time they try something new, they will have the satisfaction of knowing that they can do it in the end with persistence. Mastery brings about feelings of confidence in their mastery, which contribute greatly to happiness in adults. Just like adults, children need to pursue their own interests, or they will not experience joy even when they succeed.

You have to cultivate healthy habits from an early age. Having lots of sleep, eating a healthy diet and doing exercise are vital for everyone's health, especially for children. Children love to move around so let your toddler run around the yard since this in itself will help with their mood and development. Also, be mindful of their need for structure. Some kids are naturally easy going, but most toddlers are happier and thrive well when they have a structured schedule and are aware of what is coming. You might also need to watch out for any disconnect between certain foods and your kid's mood. You might find that, while sugar can boost your kid's energy, it can also bring aggressive behavior and/or mood swings. Your child's moods and behavior may also be influenced by sensitivities and food allergies.

As they grow older, you can also teach them the beauty and satisfaction in helping others; it doesn't have to be big, but after all, charity begins at home. Finding meaning in their lives can also make them feel less depressed in life. You can start by encouraging them to help with the household chores such as collecting their cluttered clothes and putting them in the hamper; this makes them feel that they are contributing.

Chapter 8: The Wounded Inner Child

Have you ever flown into a rage, shouting at your friends or family? Maybe you find yourself constantly manipulating, subtly trying to guilt your partner into doing things they don't want to do? Perhaps you slam your fist down on your laptop in a fit of frustration at work? After these bursts of emotion, we often feel shamed, guilty, and sheepish. "I'm a fully grown adult," you think, "and I just threw a tantrum like a toddler." John Bradshaw calls these moments **spontaneous age regressions,** moments when we return, suddenly and uncontrollably, back to the emotional mindset of a child (Bradshaw, 2013). Spontaneous age regressions are embarrassing at best, and life-ruining at worst. They may seem like they come out of the blue. We may have diagnoses and clinical names for these strange moments of childish behavior – anger management issues, anxiety disorders, co-dependence, etc. Feeling frustrated, humiliated, and out of control, we may try to self-medicate with drugs and alcohol. But these moments do not indicate that there is something "wrong" with you – this a sign that your Inner Child is wounded. When we are traumatized as children, that hurt child continues to live on inside of us, bursting out in moments of vulnerability and danger.

Children who have experienced trauma often develop behavioral "problems." Manipulating, lying, hiding things, and stealing things are often stigmatized as delinquent behaviors, but for the traumatized child, these behaviors are survival techniques rooted in self-protection (Schooler and Smalley, 2010).

Childhood trauma impacts growth in almost every way – coordination, ability to learn, social skills, physical size, and even neurologically. The behavior issues that the child develops in order to protect itself manifest in adults as attachment issues, violence, depression, anxiety, trouble with focus and learning, and anger issues (Purvis and Cross, 2007).

Chapter 9: What Do You Understand By Sensory Signals

The first and foremost thing to understand here is "what are sensory signals". The surrounding and the environment have a major role to play in a child's behaviour. Any kind of behavioural change or reaction that you may notice in your child towards this surrounding or environment is the best way to describe sensory signals. The signals would be seen in the form of a drastic change in the child's communication or interaction with people. Instead of getting panic or pressurised and creating havoc for yourself and the child, it is better to understand the sensory signals and act in a matured manner.

In this kind of a situation as a parent or an adult you should try to understand the child and create a natural and enriched environment which will ease out your child. Your main concentration should be to ensure that the surroundings are comfortable for the child. To make this possible, you should make use of the right kind of sensory strategies and tools. It is very important for you to understand that you can make the things right for your child if and only if you are at ease. You, yourself have to stop getting conscious and bugged in front of the people as this can make things more difficult for your child.

You should avoid giving increased auditory inputs or verbal commands to your child in front of people or strangers as far as possible. Try understanding and respecting the feelings of your child and honour to be real. As much as you are aware of your child's sensory signals, he or she is equally aware of the same. Remember that he or she is not doing it for pleasure or deliberately. This is the body's reaction to an uncomfortable or unfavourable surrounding or environment.

Every child is different and unique. No two kids can have the same reaction or response to the same situation. You need to understand your child well and deal with the situation in an individualistic manner. In the further chapters I will try to cover as many Sensory Signals as possible that I came to know through my research process.

Chapter 10: The 24/7 Job

You have the most important job in the world. You are a parent. It can be one of the hardest jobs, but one of the most rewarding as well. When it comes to your child you are more important than the President is to America. Teachers and educators have the second most important and toughest job. Educators have to teach the angel or monster that you have raised. Discipline has changed in schools so educators are much more hands off now. This is why it is pivotal that you as a parent teach your kid how to behave in all settings, especially school.

Parenting is a tough job and there is no parenting manual out there when you have a child. You do the best that you know how, but what happens when the best of your knowledge is not enough to help your child achieve in life? Time to take a step back from immediate reactions and look for helpful resources. This book is made to help parents better themselves so they can better their children.

Working in adult education, elementary education, and coaching various ages of athletes I have learned a lot. I have analyzed some key activities that will help groom your child to be ready to achieve success throughout life. I have seen the pain from parents, teachers, and administrators when a child is troubled. I do not believe most kids are bad, though there are some who can be purposely defiant. Most kids who seem to get in trouble a lot, are who I refer to as troubled kids. There are a lot of reasons a child could be troubled.

Home life is usually the biggest factor in a child being troubled. There are also some external factors that may not include the immediate home life. In this book we will focus on the home environment because it is the most important place for a child's behavior, attitude, and growth. Teachers and school administrators can only do so much without strong support from the home environment. The most important form of education is going to come from home. This education does not involve educational books but it revolves around your guidance for your child. Things you say and don't say to your child have a major impression upon them that you may not realize. If you are committed to helping your child or any child be the best that they can be, then this book is for you. This short guide might require you to change the way you act, speak, and think so be prepared to be challenged.

Chapter 11: Understanding Your Child

Identifying the myth of the 'bad kid.'

There's something parents of children with special needs often get tired of hearing and that is having a misbehaving child being criticized somewhere. It is painful to hear your parenting criticized in such a way. It's even more painful to hear your child's struggles dismissed so cruelly. Because there's no blood test or brain scan for mental health diagnoses and learning disabilities, some self-styled experts claim these disorders simply don't exist.

Parenting is no easy job. It's a nonstop recipe for guilt and most parents question themselves. Which means that most also question whether the problem is the child's diagnosis or their parenting. So how can you tell the difference between a discipline problem and a mental health diagnosis? Knowing the difference can help ease your parental guilt, inspire you to seek help for a struggling child, and offer peace of mind that you're making good parenting choices.

Some parents worry about their children being bad or difficult. Many people will dispute and insist that your child is being manipulative or willful. Time is here where the myth is to be dispelled.

Children usually got behavior and their behavior is driven by three things which are:

Due to enjoyment of the behavior or what comes to them after the behavior. This is why you find your child staying up to do something fun for him or her like stealing cookies

Also they do way in order to communicate something to the parent.

Children do have some behavior at times due to their emotions. For example a child may cry in bed just to manage the anger in him or she or the loneliness the kid has.

Another thing that really disturbs a parent is how to diagnose your child of mental health. Parents has to never worry. Children do have a behavior for a reason which might be due to the reasons listed above. Most parents will think they are bad, NO, you aren't neither your kid is bad. The simple way to identify the difference between a kids with behavioral issues with a child with mental issue is just looking at the child's behavior in the context of the kid's environment.

Parents need some few questions running behind their mind:

Do you understand what the kid is trying to communicate? Do the kid's behavior have some sense to you in the environment he or she is? How does your kid manage his or her feelings by her own?

Children's environment and his or her associates makes up your child's behavior and as a parent if the child in such an environment shows a behavior which gives some sense, promote her while the child showing behavioral issues in a certain environment needs you as a parent to minimize the environment to which your child stays.

EXPERT'S INSIGHT

Great strategies to model your kid's behavior are similar to the day's function for example when having a broken table, you will require a carpenter to repair. When some behavioral change is observed from your child you would require with maybe the pediatrician or a therapist. Likewise you may need to do some inquiries from the class teacher on classroom work and progress and some changes in classroom behavior if they are observed.

Ask child behavior experts on the cause of child change in behavior and if they are realistic since your child could be unable to talk freely and communicate feelings, concern is needed from expertise.

Check into the age of your child and concerning the details from behavior expertise and compare if they make some sense.

Children might get some behavior from fellow friends in school or maybe in the estate or village. As a parent you are required to identify your child's friends and his or her friend's behaviors in the estate

CHILD HOBBIES

Hobbies are not only for children fun but also help in modelling children mentally and mostly behavioral being. With the fact that people grow with spectacular talents and hobbies which model their behavior.

Many kids got varying talents and hobbies and you won't deny kids their hobbies but instead consider stepping in and offering some guidance and support.

Some tips are to guide parents on helping kids on pointing out some hobbies and ideal personalities.

Generate conducive environment for your child

There are some necessary environment to build your kids hobby to grow and develop to a great person. For example, a kid with soccer hobby will definitely require the parent to buy a ball to the kid.

You will require to designate your kid space for him or her to engage in his or her hobby, identify all the resources which will make your child develop his or her talent.

Conduct in conversation about talents and hobbies with your kid

Kids cannot articulate to their hobbies and thus as a parent you need to introduce many hobbies and thoughts since the child has many things running through their mind and providing optional thoughts could bring out the kids mind and get more associated to some thought.

Children not only require hobbies for fun but also it would be recommended that the optional thoughts given to the child would make him or her physically fit and definitely behaviorally good.

The hobbies you recommend to your child should also be inspired by your kid's personalities

CHILD ABILITIES

Is your child able to communicate openly? Is your child able to do normal work and play well? Many parents with disable kids would shed tears when seeing their kids unable to do some tasks.

It's time to never get emotionally down. Scientifically, every child has an ability hidden in him or her. Whether disabled or not, children have different abilities. Identifying a child's ability is taking time with your kid, talking and happily sharing ideas. As a parent you will closely note the child's talk lie in one part and it is your task to identify the kid's ability and empower it.

Identifying an ability is not a one day job, neither is it easy but by following some tips provided below:

Taking your child to places he or she loves and you know would empower the kid to develop a talent

Pay attention to what the children like to do and try to empower what the like to do

Set your kid high goals and encourage him or her that the goals are just easy to get and provide steps on how to achieve goals

Chapter 12: Cooking

One of the biggest fears that we as parents have about releasing our children out into the big wide world is that they will starve. When we next see them they will have faded away and resemble a skeleton - all skin and bones. Without our knowledge and guidance, that they have received until this point in their lives, they might not know what to eat, how to prepare it, or when to do so. Teaching your child to feed themselves is therefore the most logical place to start building confidence in our children to leave the nest and become functioning adults.

Cooking at Home

It is essential to teach your child some basics of cooking before they leave home. Under your watchful eyes you can instruct them on some of the most basic culinary skills, making sure that they do not injure or poison themselves on the first attempts. By learning some basics of cooking you can gain confidence in their safety and feel good in the knowledge that your child will not **need** to be reliant on restaurants for every meal.

What we want to achieve is:

Basic culinary skills and kitchen safety - e.g. sharpening knives, turning off the grill or oven, washing chopping boards after use

Knowledge of what can make you sick - how to tell if chicken is cooked, how long you can refrigerate meats and fish before throwing it out, washing vegetables to remove pesticides

Having a repertoire of at least 3 fool proof recipes that your child can make unassisted

Suggested Steps to Achievement

To achieve this I personally devised a system that in the month before my children were to leave for university (I had the luxury of knowing the exact date). This plan forced each child to cook 2 nights per week.

On a Tuesday night I would cook but they had to help. This involved preparing all of the ingredients, reading the recipes out to me as we went (even though I had done it many times before), and then helping me serve and clean up.

Then on the Wednesday night it was their turn to cook the same meal again, only this time it was on their own. I would make sure that either myself of my husband was home and right next to the kitchen in case there were any questions or minor disasters occurring so that we could guarantee that we would actually have dinner to eat.

From my experiences with my own children I know some teenagers will love and some will hate cooking. Everyone is different. Some kids will have questions, some will want to be left on their own, some will want to add of change recipes, and others couldn't care less what they are eating. At the end of the day however, your child should be confident in their own ability to complete every step of the process preparing a meal.

Start with 3 simple recipes.

It is up to you which meal ideas you want to go with, I personally taught both of my children how to make the following:

Chicken curry

Spaghetti with meatballs and tomato sauce

Steak or sausages with mashed potatoes and vegetables

All three of these are quick and easy to prepare, will not break the bank, and are relatively nutritious when using good ingredients.

If you want to find such recipes online head to http://www.taste.com.au/recipes/collections/15+minute+meals it is a website I personally use for quick and easy meal ideas.

Key Takeaways

When your child is leaving the house print the recipes you have chosen out and give them a copy. Laminate it, email, or txt them if you have to. Whatever you think is necessary to keep the recipe handy in case they need to look back over any of the steps required.

By completing this routine or a similar one to instill the essentials of cooking to your child you are helping them to become self-reliant. It will win them brownie points for their abilities when living with other people, give them confidence in their self, and potentially save money. It also instills in them the sense of family before leaving. All of which will give you confidence to let them go out on their own without you having to worry.

Food shopping

Shopping is a very practical skill that your kids should learn before they leave home. If your children have always had their food purchased for them, then having to source their own food can come as a big wake up call. It is crucial that they know where to shop, how to plan for meals, as well as rough budgeting for weekly food allowances.

What we want to impart to your child is:

Knowledge of supermarkets, vegetable stores, butcheries, and other specialty stores that you might frequent

An appreciation needs vs wants when shopping to a budget

An understanding of rough shelf life of products to determine how much to buy and how frequently

The benefit of buying in bulk for some items.

Suggested Steps to Achievement

Step 1: Meal Plan

Sit down with your child and plan out meals for the week. Set a budget and on a piece of paper or your computer draw up a weekly meal plan. An example of what this might contain is:

Monday:

Breakfast - Cereal and milk

Lunch - Sandwiches with ham, cheese, and tomato

Dinner - Spaghetti and meatballs

Snacks - Leftovers/crackers and cheese

This would be repeated for every day of the week with exceptions for days where you plan to go out for meals or have parties and things to attend. When you are doing this with you child make it clear that you will still be cooking while they are at home, but that it is important to have a clear plan when going to the supermarket.

Note: An online template for such meal planners that I use can be found at http://myexceltemplates.com/tag/weekly-meal-planner/

Step 2: Shopping List

Once you know what you want to be eating, encourage your child to draw up a shopping list. Go through what you have in the cupboards at home and can use during the week for the meals. Then have your child write a list of what you require.

This again can be done on paper, on computer, or on a phone. There are numerous apps that work for this these days including the basic 'notepad' that can be found on every iPhone.

Step 3: Let them take you shopping

This is the most important aspect when teaching your child the lesson of shopping - you need to empower your child to be responsible for the shopping. Give them the list and the plan, you are just along for the ride. Of course you will be giving helpful hints along the way to steer them in the right direction, but the final say will come down to them.

In my experience giving my own children the cash that I have budgeted for the weeks shopping in advance is a really good way to instill responsibility for the task. You can give advice, but at the end of the day they are responsible for making sure that they are not over budget. Your child will have the power to purchase the goods that they want.

Once you have done this once or twice with your child send them out to do the shopping on their own. They will probably forget some things and come back with some items that you don't expect, but that is all part of the learning process.

Note: If you are not comfortable giving your teenager money and trusting them to do the shopping then don't. Whether you do or not is to be determined by you based on your judgment and knowledge of your child.

Key Takeaways

By teaching your child all that you know about food shopping and meal planning you are empowering them to make their own choices. Learning how to shop with your guidance can potentially save your child embarrassment and money by steering them clear of products, quantities, and prices that they should avoid.

Having confidence in your child to be able to plan their own meals and buy their own food gives you one less thing to worry about once they leave the house. It also has the added benefit of taking a potential chore off of your plate during this training process. In my case once I had taught my oldest to do the shopping, my youngest child was called straight up to action and was doing most of the shopping a year before she left for university. If you get onto this lesson early enough your children could be doing the same.

Chapter 13: Child Development Phases

There are many different types of child development stages that a child will go through. While most child development stages are noticeable some are not. It is important to know what child development stages you should expect your child to go through. Doctors and other child health professionals use a chart that will predict when a child should develop certain skills.

If your child doesn't develop a certain skill by a certain time, watch your child carefully. If after another couple of months your child doesn't develop a certain developmental stage, they may actually examine your child further to rule out conditions such as autism and other disorders that can affect a child reaching child development stages.

The first year of life is critical and your child will go through many stages before completing the first year. Within the first four months of life, your child will learn to recognize you, smile, laugh, cry, and begin making sounds in an attempt to communicate. Other milestones include rolling over, sitting up, and eventually crawling and walking.

Around the twelve month mark, your child will begin to form their first words which will develop as they grow. They will create their own word list and grow that list as they get older. Language and socialization is important during this stage in life.

Between the ages of eighteen and twenty-four months, you will notice that your child's speech is very clear now and they are beginning to develop coordination and can jump without falling. He or she is also able to control their own movements more. You can begin toilet training your child during this stage.

During the ages of twenty-five to thirty-six months, your child will have clear speech and learn how to perform daily tasks to take care of themselves. This includes brushing their teeth and more.

By age three, your child has developed their personality, can identify patterns, shapes, colors, and size, and can socialize well with others.

There are other important milestones that help to complete their way of thinking so they can make decisions on their own. You can encourage this type of independence by allowing your child to choose their own outfit, shoes, or make other choices to help them become their own person.

The age of four is a critical time because this is when they must get ready for school. They should be able to count up to ten and be able to write their first name, know the real names of everyone in their family, and be working on their home address and telephone number.

At the age of five years old, a child will be ready for school, know the difference in yesterday, today, and tomorrow will be able to pronounce over 13,000 words.

Again it is important to note that not every child reaches milestones at the same exact time. Every child is different and should be treated as such. When you compare your child's progress to another, and most parents will do that, it is important to recognize what your baby is already able to do and encourage your child to keep going.

There are many different kinds of stages a child goes through from birth to adolescence; the normal stage, social-emotional and intellectual stage. These stages are also divided according to age group; they are early childhood age, middle childhood and adolescence age.

Though the boundaries of these stages shift over time, as researchers find new understandings of how a children develop as the times changes.

1. The Three Broad Stages of Child Development (Physical)

Early Childhood - from birth to 8 years

This is the fast-paced stage of child development in terms of all the areas of development; physical and mental. On the physical aspect, a child doubles his height and quadruples his weight from birth to 3 years of age.

The body proportions also shift during this stage as the head of the infant that comprises a quarter of the total body length will be in total proportion with his body as he becomes a toddler. At 3 to 8, they look like little adults already.

Middle Childhood - from 8 to 12 years

Although physical growth is steady and somewhat slow from 8 to 11 years of age, at the onset of puberty by 12, new body changes will occur. Actually the start of puberty differs individually. Some start as early as 9 while others as late as 12. Girls tend to develop earlier than boys.

Adolescence - 12 to 18 years

This is another period of rapid growth acceleration. During this period a child can grow up to 4 to 7 inches in height and about ten pounds per year. This fast growth is characterised by the hormonal growth that occurs during these years.

In some cultures, adolescent never exists or if it does, it's for a short period of time; because it coincides with their tradition of being matured adults at early ages. In some cultures the women are married by the time they reach 15, so no time to be adolescent and be the an instant adult.

2. The Social-Emotional Stage of Child Development

Early Childhood

From birth to the first year, a child's social-emotional development mainly stays within the circle of his family. After the first year to about 3 years, a child already acknowledges other people presence around him. He interacts a little and expresses his needs.

From 5 to 8 years, a child is better at expressing his feelings can by now start demanding for attention. This is the time when tantrums begin to become a big problem for parent.

Middle Childhood

Between the ages 8 to 12, a child is more socially and emotionally developed. This is due to the fact that they are more exposed to the outside world because of school. This is the time when they learn to make friends and get emotionally involved with people other than their families.

Adolescence

This is the most crucial time for social and emotional develop of every child. This is when they are heavily burdened with peer pressure and being emotionally involved with the different sex. This is also the time when they communicate much with their families as they try to create identities of their own. This is the most frustrating time for most parents.

3. Stages of Child Development in the Intellectual Aspect

Early Childhood

Intellectually, this stage is important as this is the sponge period in every child's life. This is the time when they will learn about everything the world can give them.

Middle Childhood

As this is the period of education, intellectually, a child learns a lot during this period of his development.

Adolescence

Intellectually, by this time a child has learn most things he must learn and he is just learns how to cultivate what he already knows.

Chapter 14: Children Without Rules Become Frustrated Adults

To raise a child is not easy. It includes providing an education on top of a healthy family environment, food and clothes, entertainment and cultural moments, security and safety. It means that parents set an example by their own lifestyles, being coherent and displaying integrity in their decisions. We can't just write down a set of rules, pin them to the refrigerator and expect our kids to follow them. It requires dedication and parents need to set aside times in their daily lives to be open for dialogue, counsel and advice, to teach the children about respect, discipline, sexuality and friendship.

Your rules will be much better understood once you learn how to listen and then provide an answer, rather than to begin preaching to children about how it should be and imposing menacing punishments.

As a parent, I have learned to close my eyes to the small errors in their lives. Being lenient with one of my kids who simply makes a mistake, while showing no forgiveness to another who doesn't seem to obey my decisions, makes it hard.

Though it would have been easier to just let them off the hook all of the time, follow the advice of some of my friends who say: "Times have changed. They need to be free to do whatever they want." I always believed that, in the long run, my kids would be thankful for my recurring answer "no" and insistent reprimands.

For some of my friends, the results were quite the opposite of what they expected. Some of their children went through severe depression, loss of interest in school and developed anti-social behaviors. I don't write this to prove anything, or to blame them for their position, but to show that there are real consequences when we neglect our duties as parents and become too friendly or too relaxed with discipline, allowing our children to do whatever they want. They are, after all, children.

I also had the same fears that they had, that my kids would fear me, more than respect or love me. I would fear the image of them growing older and becoming independent, thinking that they would never come back to see me, or would eventually dump me in a retirement home. I feared that my kids would look at me as I looked at my own parents. But, it was the discipline that we enforced that eventually grew our family ties stronger.

The greatest time of trial for developing a disciplined family and keep us laughing together in times of fun, was when my husband lost his job. He started working part-time and I had to find myself something to do to pay the bills. I ended up serving tables in a local restaurant. This was nothing that I didn't like and I really enjoyed it. This gave me the time to see neighbors and chit-chat for a few minutes while serving them, eat great food for free, have free drinks and get family discounts.

During that time, my kids were brought up by their grandparents. My husband and I ended up trying to compensate for the time we didn't spend with them during the week or even at weekends, and allowed them to do almost anything, trying to buy whatever we could for them. We didn't have time to follow them closely in their school progress, or even to listen to them when they had any issues.

I understand that this is a common problem for parents. Unfortunately this is a problem which is too common these days. The solution we found was to have more regular meetings with their teachers, email and call them once in a while. The teachers were not bothered at all; some really welcome the initiative on our part. We also made it clear to our in-laws what the rules of the house were, and insisted that these would extend to when they were looking after the children their own house. Our own parents understood and complied with watching our kids more carefully, helping them out by asking questions, showing interest and listening to them.

Of course, they would always relay the problems and issues to us, the parents, for a final decision. But, this way, our kids never felt abandoned and appreciated the fact that we took extra steps and efforts to make sure that they were okay. In the beginning, it sounded a bit like we were imposing an Orwellian surveillance system, but with time they came to understand.

When we had free time, we would make sure that we spent it with them. Sometimes we would help them when they were studying for their exams, other times we had fun together in the local mall or took advantage of my family discount card. It was tiring, so very tiring, but rewarding for all of us.

We were extra careful about their online habits, especially because our own parents didn't know much about computers and new technologies. We ourselves would ask questions about what they did online and shared our own discoveries on YouTube, a popular blog that we liked to read or something else that would be interesting. Nowadays, it is extremely dangerous to not know what kids are involved in when they use the Internet because this can have an impact of their lives.

We never said "no" to a party invitation from their friends, although we would always take them to the party location and pick them up afterwards, or ask any of the parents of other kids who had been invited to do it for us, as we would do for them. At a certain point in our lives, we started to "recruit" other parents to helps us out, to help each other in educating and bringing up our children in a safe environment among friends, school mates and neighbors. It's vital that you create a strong network so children feel safe.

If you are not there for them, your kids will eventually fill in the empty space of your presence as a parent, educator and friend, with other people, other resources. Most will think that they are smarter than you, until they are caught in the habits that parents would prefer them to avoid. Kids are always put under pressure to conform with their peers, whether referring to smoking, drinking or even smoking their first joint.

So, to be a friend to your child means to be present, to let the child know that you care, that the child is important and you would do anything you could to make sure that they succeed in whatever it is that they want in life. Allow them to understand the true meaning of friendship. They need to understand that their best friend is not the one that always agrees with their demands, and to recognize this as a sign that those people don't really care.

Conflicts will be less if there is this open relationship with your children, and with your partner. If your children open up to you after school about their problems, their crushes, their difficulties or their achievements, listen attentively to them. Often, they are not looking for an answer; they just want to talk about their lives. Don't push yourself to be that answer, if you don't know the whole story or you are not comfortable with responding to them. Give yourself time to research or pass it on to someone else who may have those answers. It can be their teacher, school principal, another family member, your family doctor or even local authorities, if the need calls for it. We, as parents, don't know everything and are learning about parenthood all of the time that we leave ourselves open to new ideas.

Don't judge children immediately by your own standards. Remember that our generations are miles apart from each other. We may still understand their human nature and what they feel, their emotions, but it can be difficult to empathize or stand in their shoes, in a social context or to know the full implications of what they are talking about. Don't make fun of them if their problems seem trivial to you. For your kids, these small problems are like death-defying issues or trying to solve a quantum physics brainteaser. Eventually, they will not talk to you anymore if your attitude is glib.

Still, you have to know how to place a dividing line between friendship and discipline. It is always great to have open and frank conversations with them, but know when to draw the line. You can listen to them, but you will always be the parent, providing insights into their issues, giving them proper balance for their problems, supporting their decisions and also correcting them when needed. Don't be afraid to do so, fearing that they will not talk to you anymore. If you don't, they will eventually ask you why you didn't warn them or advise them properly.

So, where do you draw the line? What is friendship and what is parenting? When do you listen and when do you speak? It is very difficult to know. As we said, all kids are different. They change, according to age. Parents are also different and their social situations vary. Even cultural backgrounds influence this formula. You will have to use your intuition and your knowledge of your kids and their circumstances and lead with your heart and mind working in sync.

Chapter 15: The Beauty Of Parenting

You can hear a lot of people both in the media and in your neighborhood complain about how their kids keep on running around, putting their fingers in electrical sockets or scribbling nonsense on walls with permanent markers they found lying around on daddy's table, infants crying at three in the morning, and pre-teens starting to get embarrassed of their parents. Although these complaints may seem to give you the impression that parenting is an extremely difficult endeavor to pursue, there are actually things that can change your opinion of it.

Parents, especially first-timers, get nervous about how they are going to take care of their child. Of course, it is completely understandable that first-time parents will feel the jitters associated with having no knowledge of what exactly should be done in particular parenting problems. Luckily, there are many resources (including this one) which can help you with whatever problems you may have with your child. However, even if you have all the things that you would need in taking care of your child properly, it would all still not work if you are not confident with what you are doing.

The first thing that you must realize as a parent is that you have been bestowed with the honor of being a parent of someone. This is a privilege that is not given to anyone, and you should be proud of it! Parenting gives you the opportunity to see someone as he or she grows up and becomes a self-sufficient and successful adult. Not only that, you actually get the chance to actually be a part of his or her journey towards that goal of becoming and adult in the future.

Secondly, you must accept the fact that you cannot do it all on your own all the time. Many parents think that they would not be able to take care of their child on their own, and feel guilty when they make even the smallest mistakes such as seeing their child trip and fall after running. As a parent, you need to be surrounded by a support system that could help you realize how much of a great parent you are by realizing the importance of seeking help from those who know better and learning from their wisdom.

Third, parenting is a job done with love. It is a vocation. Parenting is when you give your heart and all of your best effort to your child for you to see her grow into a beautiful and independent person. The reason why parenting is a satisfying although tiring job is that what you are doing basically involves taking care of a person whom you will love for the rest of your life. Their small achievements in life, from learning how to walk for the first time to starting to go to school, are the greatest moments that you can definitely tell yourself that you have been a part of, and that is definitely saying something. A relationship that is tightly bonded in love never becomes exhausting, and it does not make you feel that you have no energy left.

Chapter 16: Helping Your Children To Socialize

In this chapter, you are going to learn the tips on how to help your children socialize. Most parents want their children to be prepared in facing the world and becoming successful.

In this event, some parents get frustrated that they take their children out to the world and force them to interact with others. What's not been taken into account is the fact that some children are naturally introvert. They don't realize their children prefer to stay inside, read books, listen to music or do individual activities rather than interact with other kids.

You cannot force your introvert child to act like an extrovert one. If you think your child loves solitude, what would be the best way to help him go out more?

Understanding Introverts

The first step in helping your introvert child to socialize is by learning more about the nature of introversion. This way, you don't worry too much when your child is acting differently from other children who are more outgoing.

As opposed to general belief, spending most of the time alone and not expressing one's feelings is not a sign of depression. Such behaviors can be a sign of emotional distress but in case of depression, you look for behavioral changes. Introverts don't respond to outward influences; they are naturally timid and silent while depressed people can be extroverts turned into introverts when exposed to tragedies that are more than they can handle.

Accept Your Child's Preferences

Once you understand the nature of introversion, you'll become aware of your child's preferences. And once you determine his preferences, you have to accept and respect his preferences. For instance, introvert children prefer to have fewer friends. When you see that your child has one or two friends while extroverts have five or more friends you might feel the need to encourage him to socialize more. You might even try to ask him what could be his "problem" with socializing.

Now that you understand introversion, you will understand that your child can be completely happy with just one friend. You will also understand that having few friends does not mean that he has social problems so you can leave him the way he is. Forcing your child to develop friendship with more children won't make him more outgoing. When you push him too much he will only feel irritated, which can make you think he has problems. So instead, you need to accept his social preferences and let him enjoy being friends with kids he loves to spend time with.

Accept His Personality

You can show your love towards your child by accepting him as he is. What would your child feel if you keep on comparing him to other children? As a parent, you want the best for your child. Because of that, it's normal that you feel the need to encourage him in making more friends if you can see him spending more time by himself than you think he should.

However, if you are starting to act like his behavior is not normal or it's becoming a problem, he may translate it in other words you don't intend. He might feel that something is wrong with him and that you can't love him because of that. He may think that why would you want him to be something that he is not if you really love him?

You need to keep in mind that some kids can be more emotionally sensitive. They may feel differently from what you feel about them. You love your child but if you keep on pushing him to become someone he is not then he might think that you don't like him. He might feel that you don't love him. So accept him as he is and like him the way you love him.

Be Supportive

As you discover your child's personality, you will begin to notice how he can be easily intimidated by others. In addition to that, people who surround him may not be able to do what's best for him. For instance, a teacher may think that he is not doing well in group activities because he doesn't interact with other students. She might be pushing your child too much to participate more in class. This is a tough situation because group activities have become necessary in education system. You want to support your child in this case but you don't want to ask the teacher to excuse him from group activities.

What you need to do here is help his teacher understand the reason why your child does not enjoy engaging in group work as much as other students. You may ask professional help from a counselor to help you explain your child's case to his teacher.

Chapter 17: Single Dad With Toddlers: Handling Temper Tantrums

After your baby has grown up to be a vibrant toddler, and just when you thought your baby has outgrown the irritating bouts of non-stop crying and flailing limbs to catch your attention, comes now the temper tantrums. This time around, it is a more serious, albeit, more violent behavioral problem you will have to face.

It can be as mild as continuous crying and whining with no signs of stopping. Or, it can be more violent and involve ear-shattering screams, breath holding, kicking, and hitting at people or objects. Not all toddlers have it of course but most of them do. And, unless your toddler is one of the rare exceptions, you better understand why toddlers have them so you'd know what to do.

Temper Tantrums and Why Kids Have Them

Temper tantrums are common among 1 to 3 year old toddlers. It is actually part of their normal development so there is no need to push the panic button. Some toddlers manifest temper tantrums on a regular basis while others rarely do. At any rate you should not view toddler temper tantrums negatively.

They are simply manifestations of their frustration in not being able to get a thing or in most cases, their parents to do something they want. And because they don't have the same inhibitions or control of an adult, they vent their frustrations with varying degrees of temper tantrums.

Basically, tantrums are the toddlers' desperate way of communicating a message across to you - like telling you they are tired, or hungry, or uncomfortable with something, or they just want your undivided attention (much like when they were still bottle feeding infants). The only difference is back then, they can only cry and flay their limbs but this time around they know how their bodies work and so they scream, and kick and hit – out of frustration.

Remember they are still learning language and so their ability to communicate is limited. What happens then is the toddlers begin to understand much more than what they are able to express in words. And their inability to communicate what they want leads to frustration which touches off or triggers the tantrums.

As toddlers discover more and more of their surroundings they develop a feeling of independence and a sense of control of everything around them. They begin to think of doing things themselves or wanting the things they fancy and start expecting to be given everything they want. And when they discover the limits to what they can do or find out they can't have everything they want frustration sets in which ultimately precipitates the temper tantrums.

The good news is as the toddler learns to communicate more effectively, and as he develops a better understanding of the things around him, his level of frustration diminishes and ultimately just fades away.

So, how should you deal with your toddler's temper tantrums?

Will you hit or spank the child? Absolutely not! Every child looks up to the father as a model of how he should behave. Clearly, hitting and spanking will only result in negative behaviors which can spill over to the future. Besides, it sends the wrong signals to the child. It creates the wrong notion that punishment and the use of force is alright.

As much as possible you should avoid the tantrums by preventing incidents from blowing into a major scene that will only frustrate the kid.

Here are some ways you can avoid incidents from developing into major tantrums.

Give him a dose of negative attention.

According to some child experts, one of the best ways to deal with temper tantrums is to ignore them - whenever possible. It may come as a shock to you but it really doesn't mean you will totally not respond to the child when he starts acting up.

It is a tactical way of ignoring then attending to the child. It is called negative attention. It involves momentarily ignoring the child (**even if he starts screaming**) until he calms down. And once he has calmed down you divert his attention by offering him something else other than what he wanted. Toddlers have very short attention span so if you offer a replacement for what he wants he is likely to forget everything else at once. This cushions and lessens the feeling of frustration that comes with not getting what he wants.

Take note though that this approach will only work if you have a strong, positive relationship with your child. To achieve this, make it a habit to praise him or reward him with attention for every positive behavior he shows. This will strengthen the positive relationship between you and your child such that when you ignore him every time he starts acting up, it won't escalate into major scene.

Make him feel he is in control.

If your child feels he has control over things he is not likely to go into tantrums. For example, instead of emphatically telling him to do something give him options. An example of this is instead of saying "take a bath now" you can try asking him "Do you want to take a bath now or would you rather do it after dinner?"

Don't push him if he has reached his limits.

If you know your child is tired, don't push him to do another thing like do an errand for you. You should know your child's limits and must not push him to go beyond that.

Accommodate whenever possible.

You may give in once in a while. You should know better when you will ignore his requests and when not to. If the request is reasonable perhaps you should give in.

Be firm if his safety is at stake.

If your child wants to do something where his safety will be compromised and starts acting up because you forbid him, don't give in. Be firm about it to make him understand that when it come to his safety you are inflexible. What you can do is hold him firmly for a while. It will send him the signal that you are not going to budge.

There are two things you must remember when your kid starts acting up. First, keep your cool. Never lose your temper or feel frustrated. Your kid will sense this and he will only be more frustrated. By staying calm you can assess the situation more clearly and take the most appropriate action for the situation.

Second, you should never reward your toddler's tantrums by giving in to his wishes. It will only make him bolder. Knowing that his tantrums work will encourage him to do it again and again to get what he wants.

Do not reward your child's tantrum by giving in. This will only prove to your little one that the tantrum was effective. Instead, verbally praise a child for regaining control.

You should not really worry much about your child's tantrums because he will stop on his own when he sees it is not getting him anything. Also, the tantrums will slowly disappear as your child matures.

Chapter 18: How To Be A Dad

If you think diapering and doting are a mother's job, you are in the wrong century. Today's father does it all. Don't fret. Wouldn't you rather be an active part of the team rather than to sit on the bench?

Coming Home

One of the most important and memorable drives you will ever make is the first one with your baby. You may be a nervous wreck, but that's fine as long as you don't have one… a wreck, that is.

Make sure to note that the hospital will not allow your baby to leave unless you have an infant car seat that meets regulations. It's advisable to check with your individual hospital long before you are pulling up to fetch mother and child.

Once you get home, you will be able to introduce your baby to his new home. Sometimes that includes older siblings and pets, so let them get acquainted safely and set some rules in place. Younger children need to know that nothing but a pacifier or bottle goes in the baby's mouth or hands as well as they need to have permission before holding him. Do make sure that siblings feel like they are valuable members of the team.

Pets will need to be watched carefully around the little one. Crying often gets on their nerves and they react differently than they normally would. Some even get jealous. It's nice to let them smell some of the baby's belongings before he comes home; once he is in the home, they can sniff him, too. Most likely, to a dog, your baby will smell like you and the baby's Mom.

You will want to keep the racket down so your little one doesn't become alarmed. If you keep moderate noise going when he is sleeping, he won't get in the habit of having to have everything silent in order to sleep well.

If you are suddenly worried about not having Dad experience, lighten up. Your baby has never been a baby. It's all good.

How to Hold Your Baby

You know how you hold a football, right? Believe it or not, there is one method to the madness that is actually called a football hold. See, you're feeling more comfortable already, aren't you?

Although you are a rookie at baby-holding right now, it is something that will eventually become second-nature to you once you get the hang of it, just like holding a football or driving your car.

The most important thing to remember is that newborns need their neck supported when they are held. The muscles are not yet developed and are weak so he cannot hold his head upright; it bobs around. To prevent whiplash and possible tearing of the muscles and ligaments, it is imperative to support his neck.

Here are some ways that you can hold your baby:

Cradle Hold. Cradle him in your arms with his head supported by the crook of one arm (located just inside your inner elbow) and his butt supported by your other arm.

Football Hold. Curl your baby around you so that his legs and feet are behind you. Draw his body around your waist or chest so that he is curled. Support his head with your hand. This can be done on one side using only one hand and arm so that it frees your other hand to give him a bottle or to take or make a phone call.

Chest and Belly Hold. Place your arm in a curled position then lay him with his belly facing the inside of your arm (meaning he is facing outward) with his neck and head supported by the inside of your elbow (the crook of your arm). This is basically a reverse "cradle hold."

Snuggle Hold. Hold your baby up next to your chest with his face turned to one side. Be sure that your shirt is not gaping, preventing him from breathing. Support his neck and head with one hand and his butt with the other. If he is upset, you can pat his butt gently and he will often calm down.

Face-to-Face Hold. When seated, lay your baby where his is supported by your legs and is facing you. Use your hands to support his neck and head.

Here are some more helpful hints for holding your all-star:

If at first you don't succeed, try, try again!

You will often get better results if you hold your little one in a direction where he can't see his Mommy.

Skin-to-skin contact is excellent therapy for the both of you.

Slings will help you hold your baby, giving you more freedom and confidence. Be sure she is in a position where she can breathe without any obstructions as some slings are rather snug.

When you are first trying out your holding patterns, chose a time of day that she is usually the happiest.

If your wife gives you pointers, don't take offense. You are your baby will get your own holds down eventually.

Feeding

Initially, your baby will be trying out a lot of new things, including feeding (drinking milk, of course). There will be decisions to make. Many will be made by your little one and will depend upon her digestive system and preferences. Some, however, will be determined by baby's Dad and Mom.

Breast or Bottle?

The benefits of breast feeding are many. According to the United Nation's Children's Fund (UNICEF), babies should be breastfed exclusively for the first six months of their lives. It is also recommended that the nursing begins within the first hour of life.

Below are some of the reasons why breastfeeding is preferred:

It is healthier.

Breastmilk contains immunities from the mother.

It is convenient.

It is less expensive than formula.

There is a special bond between mother and baby.

It is all-natural.

It aids in preventing sudden infant death syndrome (SIDS).

It contains protein, calcium and other nutrients.

It is easily digested.

It contains important fatty acids.

It promotes your baby's brain development.

Breastfeeding can help prevent obesity later in life.

It helps Mom lose weight easier.

But, there is also formula if breast feeding isn't working for Mom and baby.

What is Formula?

Some parents chose to use formula, while others have to use formula because the mother cannot nurse well for some reason; the baby cannot/will not nurse or has digestive issues that does not tolerate breastmilk.

The good news is that there are a lot of choices when it comes to formulas these days. There are regular types as well as soy and organic. For the little ones with big digestion issues, there are even predigested formulas.

One advantage to opting for formula is that you will get to play a bigger role in the feedings. Another is that it frees the baby's Mom to go back to work or just to take some time off to shop, take a long bath or whatever else she may want to do. Some say that bottle fed babies sleep for longer intervals, which is a good thing.

Here are some facts on formulas:

There is no need to heat the formula.

You can get baby bottles that have disposable bags for air-free feeding with no mess, no sterilization.

If your baby sips from the formulation, it needs to be discarded after the feeding. Otherwise, it can be saved until the next time of feeding.

It is not a good idea to get low-iron types unless approved by your baby's pediatrician.

Soy is generally not recommended.

There are many formulas. You can get pre-made ones, meaning you don't even have to add water. If you use a powder version, make sure you use purified water to make the bottle.

Burping Baby

You don't want your little one to get gassy. Babies tend to get air when they gobble up their milk. It's important to burp your baby each time he eats.

In a sitting position, hold your baby to your chest with his chin resting on your shoulder and your hand behind his neck for proper support. Or, you can hold him in your lap with him across your knees, looking down. You can also sit him up on your lap, supporting his head and neck with one hand.

Rub and gently pat his back. Do so until he produces a burp. It may take a while, but it will be well worth it for him to NOT get gas.

How to Burp a Baby

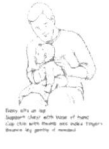

Important Steps with Your Baby

Diaper Duty

Unless you just completely luck out, you will be asked to change a diaper at some point. Or, you may not even be given much choice. If your baby is in your care and poops or pees, don't be one of "those" Dads who hand the baby back to Mom or even waits until she gets back home if she happens to be out.

Here are some simple steps to diapering:

Lay your baby in a safe place, such as a changing table.

Take the diaper off by unsticking the tab on each side by the baby's hips.

If you are changing a little boy, be careful you don't get sprayed.

If there is poo, gently wipe it off baby with the diaper as best you can and then wad the "surprise" inside the diaper.

Never leave your baby unattended while you dispose of a diaper. It's best to have a little diaper genie or trash next to the changing table.

Finish the cleaning with a baby wipe or clean, wet, warm cloth.

Lift baby's bottom up and lay the back of the new fresh diaper under him so the inside of the diaper faces his bottom. The back of the diaper comes up higher just like pants do.

Bring the diaper up between his legs and then cover his front side.

Fasten both sides with the built-in adhesive tape flaps.

Pat yourself on the back for a Daddy-job well done!

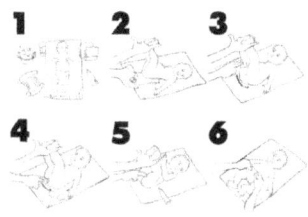

Bathing Your Baby

Relax. It's not nearly as scary as you are thinking it will be. She won't melt. Simply undress your baby and lay her on a baby bath sponge or infant bath tub. Then gently wash her using your hand or a baby washcloth. Be sure to use soap that is designated for babies, preferably organic and for sensitive skin, to be on the safe side. Rinse her with cups of lukewarm water and pick her up and bundle her in a soft, dry towel. See how easy that was?

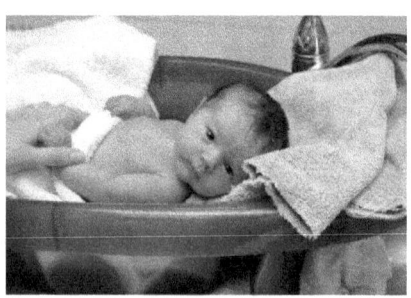

Dressing Your

Little Darling

The object of the game is to get the baby's clothing on her while supporting her head and as comfortably as possible.

Here's one way to dress your little child. Support your baby on your lap. If the neckline of the outfit doesn't snap, button or zip, be sure to stretch it to ease over her head. Gently put your hand in the sleeves from the wrist upwards toward the shoulder in order to grasp her hand and pull it through the wrist hole. You can maneuver her legs into the outfit the same way as well. Just remember that she won't be able to "help you" so you'll have to totally do it, usually with her wiggling and drawing her legs up, clenching her fists and so forth. Undressing is the same in backward motion.

Crying, Colic and other Calamities

You might as well face the facts. Your baby is going to cry a lot. It's unnerving at best for such a pint-size being to be so fretful and you have no clue why or what to do.

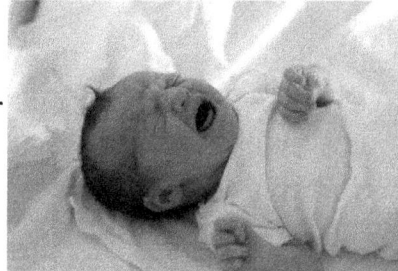

Often, it's not that hard to figure out though if you know the signs.

Some common reasons for crying are:

She is hungry.

Her tummy hurts due to gas or maybe even colic.

She needs to burp.

Her diaper is wet or dirty and needs a diaper change.

She is bored.

She is lonely.

She is in pain.

She is not feeling well but isn't exactly in pain.

She is sleepy.

Here are some things you can do:

Hunger. Feeding her is the ultimate answer if she is hungry, but you don't want her to eat if she's not hungry and get a tummy ache so it's good to be as sure as possible. Figure how long it has been since her last feeding and calculate. Take into consideration about how much she ate or how long she nursed. Lip smacking, turning her head to one side (known as rooting) and putting her hands in her mouth are good indications she is hungry.

Sleepy. Babies tend to fight sleep, meaning they are sleepy but don't want to give in to it. You can try rocking, singing and soothing; eventually, she will most likely fall asleep if there's not another underlying issue.

Wet or Dirty. Change her! If her bottom is irritated, you may give her doctor a call and describe the rash.

Over or Under Stimulated. Of course if you know which it is, you can play with her… or not. Don't get too worried about this one though. Even adults suffer from boredom or being overwhelmed. Do what you can but the situation will soon take care of itself.

Gas. Making sure to burp your baby good is one way to help prevent little gas bubbles, but if you suspect that is what is wrong with her, hold her over your shoulders and gently rub and pat her back. You can do the same with her over your legs when you are sitting down. Basically, you do what you do after a feeding.

Colic. Colic is an ongoing tummy ailment. For centuries, it has had babies and parents alike in tears. Clues are if your baby cannot be consoled and begins crying at the same time a day or night or right after a feeding. Drawing his legs up is another sign. Gripe water is a natural solution you may try or your pediatrician may have another recommendation.

Chapter Takeaways

It may be a little stressful the day your your baby comes home for the hospital but don't worry, things will fall into place.

Being depressed is natural, for mother and fathers. If one of you gets too down, it's time to talk to a professional.

Holding your baby skin-to-skin is therapeutic for you and him.

Do all the extra things you can around the house. It will make both you and the baby's mom feel better and it's a good measure your relationship as well.

It's just a fact of life that babies cry, but knowing what to look for can help you figure it out and hopefully solve the problem.

Chapter 19: What's With 'No!'?

Every parent goes through it, and the first time they hear the word from their adorable toddler, they automatically think, "Oh no, it's the Terrible Twos. We've reached that milestone."

It's all right; every parent goes through this stage with their child because it's an absolutely normal phase of development. However, that doesn't mean you have to suffer for very long. There are many ways you can help your child get through this very emotionally charged period of their life.

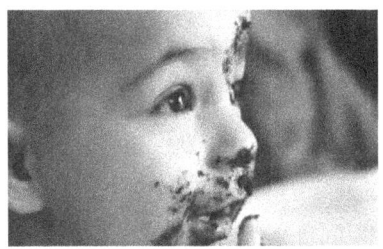

The technical term for this fascination with the word 'no' is known as refusal to child psychologists, and the simple fact is your toddler is saying this word just because they can. Your toddler's discovered they have a will, and they want to exercise it to the best of their ability, which means saying 'no' to the one person who has told them what to do their entire life – you.

It probably seems this phase has come on overnight, and it really does happen suddenly, leaving you confused as to why your child has suddenly become defiant. Thankfully, the stage can disappear as quickly as it came on, and you're left with the 'I don't know' or 'Maybe' stage. However, while you're waiting for your toddler to make it through this stage, you can experiment with a few coping strategies to make it a little easier.

Offer Your Toddler Choices

In reality, this is all your toddler is asking for. They're in the mood to make their own decisions rather than have Mom and Dad play tyrant, so play nice and give them a few choices! For example,

Do you want juice or milk today?

Do you want to wear the purple or pink shoes?

Do you want to play nice with your friend, or do you want to play alone?

Do you want to wear the pants or the skirt?

Just make sure you don't offer your toddler more than two options, and never offer them an option you don't want to follow through with. If you don't want them to wear the red shoes, then don't offer them. If your toddler is indecisive, counting is a good motivator, too: "I'm going to count to five and then you choose something, or I'm going to choose for you."

You have to be careful with how often you use this option because your toddler will become immune to it eventually.

Offer an Appearance of Options

There are moments where you can't offer your toddler another option, so you have to offer the appearance of one. To do this properly, you need to keep two important things in mind: you know more than your child does, and just about anything can be turned into a choice. Let's look at some examples.

"Would you like to stay in the car for two minutes and play or get out of the car now?" Either way, your child is going to end up getting out of the car.

"Would you prefer we put the sweater on backward or frontward?" Since both of you understand your child most likely won't want to wear the sweater backward, you're adding some humor to the situation. However, if your child says they want to wear it backward, then you need to let them wear it backward. Never go back on a choice when they've made it.

Start Teaching Other Responses

One of the reasons your toddler is saying this word so much is because they don't know a lot of other words, and you've most likely said this one to them a lot.

Help your toddler expand their vocabulary by turning the word 'no' into a game.

When your toddler says 'no,' ask him or her what the opposite of 'no' is. When he or she says 'no,' ask them what comes in between 'no' and 'yes,' and if they don't know, tell them – maybe, perhaps, and possibly. If your toddler has a tendency to say 'no' rudely, then have them say 'no, thank you' instead. And for the chatty toddlers out there who say 'no' rudely, have them say 'no, thank you very much.'

You could make their 'no' response a little less automatic and possibly get a yes if you set up the situation with something silly, such as asking your child, "What would a dog say if you said, 'Mr. Dog, would you want a bone?'" When your toddler says, "Yes," you'd follow up with, "And what would you say if I asked you if you wanted to eat your peas?" Hopefully, your toddler will be giggling enough that he or she will be too happy to rebuff the peas.

Limit Your Use of the Word 'No.'

Your toddler might be screaming 'no' at the top of their lungs all the time because he or she is constantly hearing that word from you, and it's most likely directed at them. If this is the cause of the issue, then you should try to use alternative words to 'no' instead.

Some examples of this might be:

Uh-uh

Nope

Nay

Nah

No way

Negative

Out of the question

Under no circumstances

Not likely

Thumbs down

Go fish

One way to do this is to use words that are more specific to the situation that's happening. For example, "We don't hit other people," or, "It's time to use your indoor voice, please."

Be Firm

There are going to be times that no matter what you do to avoid or distract your toddler from the situation, you'll end up in a showdown. If your toddler stops in the middle of the street and refuses to move any further, you'll move your toddler quickly. But safety concerns aren't the only reason to be firm with a toddler. A toddler has a will, but you can't allow your toddler to exert that will all the time. It'll get messy very quickly.

It's perfectly fine for you, as a parent, to say, "This isn't a time when I can give you an option. There're no options now. I know you don't want to do this, or you don't like this, and I'm sorry about that, but this is the way it has to be." And when your toddler asks why, you respond with, "Because I'm your mommy/daddy."

Despite all these strategies, you'll still have to wait out this stage. Thankfully, it won't last forever, and with some of these strategies in place, it'll be a little less of a time period before you get back into the swing of agreeing with each other.

Chapter 20: Brain And Emotional Development Of Children. And How Can You Use It.

Brain and Mental development of Children Ages 18 months - 2 years.

Curiosity and investigation are the main activities of children during this period. Of particular interest to them is that which is forbidden. You will do the best service to your child if you limit his activities as little as you can. And only when the child could be hurt.

In this period, fear is generated sudden and unexpected situations from the environment. This may be the fear of separation, which is also called separation anxiety and is the result of an ever-increasing association of the child with the parents and understanding of what separation is.

When a child turns two, there is a development of shame and guilt, which are often interconnected. For example, if the child is without a diaper and gets caught, he or she may feel ashamed.

Speech develops fastest during this period. The child's vocabulary increases to about 100 words. The child develops a steady interest in things in his or her environment, pointing at them, as well as asking questions about everything. When a child adopts about 50 words, your baby begins to interconnect words in simple sentences.

Brain and Mental development of Children Ages 2 years - 3 years.

The common opinion on toddlers is that they are exhausting. However, if we help them discover the world around them, everyone will profit—both parents and children. During this year of life, the child experiences an accelerated intellectual, social, and emotional development. Not only does your toddler meet the world around him/her, but he/she is also learning its meaning.

A dancer, architect, painter, athlete, or animal imitator—the child is learning to play all of these roles. Among these new skills, they also might have learned to throw items in a certain direction. Your toddler knows how to catch a ball, jump like a rabbit, walk on his/her fingers forward or backward, or jump over an obstacle 5 cm high. In this period, children get a sense of rhythm and might play when they hear music.

A child at this age is very active, curious, restless, and reluctant to have limitations. Your toddler will test the limits to find which behavior is acceptable, as well as to find out how much power he or she has over adults. Your toddler wants to be alone, but still needs help from adults. In this period, relations with parents, other family members, and acquaintances are changing.

The child's vocabulary now has 300 words from which he knows to formulate simple and grammatically correct sentences. Your toddler will constantly ask questions that begin with "what" or "who." More and more, your child will enjoy poetry and stories.

In the third year of age, it becomes interesting for a child to play by imitating various adult activities. This game triggers the imagination. Inexhaustible objects become living entities, immovable things begin to move. It's all about imagination!

Brain and Mental development of Children Ages three - four years.

Three-year-olds and four-year-olds, are very versatile in movement. They run smoothly, bounce, walk on their fingers, and climb the stairs using alternating steps. Walking backwards and riding a tricycle is are real challenges.

From the age of three years onward, children become more skilled in everyday activities: eating with a spoon and fork, washing, dressing, and going to the bathroom. They become more tactile and skilled with their hands, but they still cannot draw with watercolors. The child can carry a bowl of water a greater distance without spilling.

Between the third and the fourth year, children develop into real little chatterboxes. Their dictionary contains about 500 words which they pronounce about 20,000 times a day.

For parents, endless repetition and the eternal "what" and "why" questions can be very tiring. But through repetition, the child is expanding his vocabulary, practicing speaking, and learning what to say in different forms and combinations.

It is important that you do not talk to your child in a childlike manner (babbling). Do not use baby talk as it will prevent the child from learning to speak properly. Whatever the child says, translate it into plain language by repeating it in its proper form. Give praise whenever the child uses the proper forms of words and sentences.

Children at this age are becoming more emotionally intelligent, which can produce many problems. The most common problems are quarrels. Quarrels between siblings and between friends are common. Just be patient.

What is important?

Remember that children are not consciously aware of their disobedience by their second year, which means the child is breaking the rules because of ignorance. For this very reason, it is very important for parents to not hurt the child and lose his or her trust. It is important to prevent physically injuring the child while he or she is still learning about the world around him or her.

When a child is three - four years old, he or she can understand the relationship between cause and effect (if I do this, this is what will happen...) and this helps them to understand why they are allowed to do some things and are not allowed to do other things.

This understanding of causes and consequences represents the first step towards the progressive adoption of family standards and the formation of what could be termed "loyalty" to their own duties and limitations. For this reason, it is only from this moment that it is possible to talk about disobedience as a conscious deviation from the set rules.

Which educational model to choose?

After the second year, it is time to tell your child the first, simple rules that will allow him to learn what's good and what's bad. After that, with the help of mother's and dad's explanations and his or her own experience, the child will understand why some behavior is positive and other behavior is not. However, the mere giving of rules is not enough for the rules to be respected, and there will often be a "conflict" with a youngster who wants to express his or her own independence just by breaking the rules.

However, the basic and most important thing is to respect the child's nature and instincts by avoiding methods which he or she doesn't understand. In this way, it is easier for parents to be always consistent in their actions and for a child to believe them when they say something.

What is the right behavior?

Here are some rules that can help you establish and maintain authority with your child:

☐Don't set too many rules: it is unrealistic to expect from a child of two - three years to act as an adult. It is better to stick to a few clear rules that are easy to respect.

☐Don't constantly change or improve the rules: children have a great memory and if your toddler is allowed today what was forbidden yesterday he or she may think that the rules are not important.

☐ Avoid requirements that need to be met instantly ("go wash your hands," "come to the table") if the child is busy with play. Commands like that are sure to cause some kind of clash and challenges which question the authority of parents. It is wisest to give the child time - "another round and then go wash your hands."

☐ When you order a child to do something your tone of voice must be firm and determined. Loss of control or yelling can scare the child and keep him in fear, but it does not contribute to authority.

☐ Praise your child when he or she is doing something good. If you yell at your child over the smallest things, he will find it harder to understand the difference between good and bad.

Punishment: yes or no?

By two years, the child is still unable to link its behavior to punishment. For this reason, the experience of being punished or the imposition of punishment will not result in the child becoming obedient.

Chapter 21: Understanding Childish Tantrums

I remember my second boy was quite a difficult child at early childhood. He was so difficult, even friends and neighbors avoided his tantrum which was in excess. It got my wife troubling and my visiting mother-in-law would impress it on my wife that some children were just different. She advised we gave him time, to get out of it. It actually came to pass.

Yet my wife wasn't encouraged by her mother's advice. I knew my wife was thinking, maybe our son had a psychological problem or so but I didn't think so. It was a big issue for her when the boy was between the ages of two years and four. My wife was down psychologically during those years. I didn't give her any indication that she was coming to a hasty conclusion, despite my assurance. It was a pleasant joy that the boy eventually stopped his rantings.

When the young man is reminded of that naughty episode today, he just smiles over the remark. (As I recall, my own younger brother who is now in his fifties, was equally difficult as a young child. He kept my parents on their toes then).

Knowing Your Children

There is also a need for direct observation to understand a growing child. I will cite an instance which was initially confusing. This happened during the second day of my younger son at school. The school was much closer home than that of his elder brother. We wanted convenience for him and us.

On that day, I noticed he wasn't excited when we dropped him at school. And I expressed my observation to his class teacher. She couldn't give me a convincing answer but otherwise she offered a wrong explanation with so much confidence. She said, that my kid, when spoken to, couldn't respond. She said the boy had a communication problem. Being new parents, I almost believed but my instinct told me otherwise.

Right there and then, I spoke to my noisy son. I asked him why he was not responding to his teacher. Alas, my boy was tongue tied! He squeezed his face, looked at all of us and refused to answer me and his mum. I could see my wife was troubled and sad momentarily. And so I was confused. The boy was simply staring into space.

Let me digress a little bit, before I conclude on this experience; why this got me confused.

This was a boy who had been stuttering to speak in such a hurry, right from his first birthday. By 18 months, he was able to complete a simple sentence. He was sure of himself. He was noisy. He would speak up to show his displeasure even to any visitor that came to our home. However, the older brother was the opposite in that respect.

As he turned two years of age, his choice of words became more matured for his age. He was fond of scolding his mum and I. We took it in our stride - as fun.

At the age of three, he questioned why my car was not a brand new car? And why my friends were richer than me? Why my car couldn't "run" faster than all the vehicles, when we were on the road? I did not have answers for him at times. We just enjoyed and cherished these knocks and as I recall this now, I cannot but smile.
But then, we cautioned him he couldn't speak to outsiders like that, that he would

be spanked by them. He was almost different from his elder brother who has been a cool chap from time. Surprisingly today, both of them as young adults, appear mellow but not without their confident and assertive nature. I suspect they got these from me.

Now back to the second day at school and the teacher's pronouncement of my son's inability to communicate.

I told the teacher I didn't have an answer of why the boy chose not to speak. That this boy, everybody knew as a talkative. I did not agree with the teacher's position. I revealed that this boy was "a parrot "at home. I told the teacher that as experts in child care, we expected a more informed solution. We, as new parents, were naive but there wasn't any further convincing explanation from the school. At that point, I felt I needed to ask my son later at home what the problem was. We left him at school that morning and went to work. The mum picked him up in the afternoon, after work.

On getting home that evening, I engaged him. The boy was his normal boisterous self and he was very ready to tell me what happened.

He said he didn't want to go to that school; that he preferred his older brother's school!
I asked why he didn't say so. He burst into laughter. He explained he wanted to be seeing his brother, in the same school, he attended. (This was the same brother he engaged in cat fights at home, whenever he was in his naughty mood). We had no choice but to enroll him in his elder brother's school. (I lost part of the fees in the previous school). He spent five years in the new school, without any problem before going passing to a high school.

For the senior son, it was similar challenge of adjustment, when he got admitted to the high school, he earlier cherished.

In the first year, he was boarded in the hostel but he never found it funny. He cried all through the months, wanting to go from home. The school was over an hour's drive in thick traffic. On monthly parental visits, he was never looking happy. He wanted to go from home.

The school was far from home. I insisted the first year must be finished in the boarding school. He lost weight. He couldn't adjust to the environment of petty bullying by some rascal seniors and the inconvenience of hostel life.

From the second year, we allowed him to go from home. My wife had to wake him up, early in the morning to catch a public bus, to meet resumption time. Much later, he had a free ride by a neighbor, who worked close to the school's location. He was happy with the new arrangement and did not mind the compromise. Towards the final year, he realized he was a senior at school (and there was nobody to bully him). We also felt the time used to commute, was eating into his study time. His final year and external examinations were around the corner. So I insisted he returned to the hostels, for his last two years to finish up. It was easier for him to accept, as he was relatively more matured now. He reasoned with me.

How Do Kids Acquire Experience?

Kids are like new sponges, ready to be soaked up. Kids are like an artist's blank canvas, waiting for the strokes of the paint. Kids are curious about everything; right from their mother's womb. I want to believe a child's initial worldview can be likened to an adult who has found himself in a new environment. The adult is consciously asking questions about the novel experience.

The new environment is engaging all the senses and he must explore and interact. By so doing, he initiates an action which could ultimately be correct or lead to failure.

Either of the experiences nurtures maturity. He makes subsequent adjustments to cope, next time. Such realizations welcome a gradual but a new experience. Indelible lessons would have been learnt. You will know the rules to abide with or not. And a child has to go through this same process but he needs an adult guide, of good character and wisdom for a positive outcome. So kids too, acquire experiences like adults in similar manner.

These are the thoughts that readily come into my mind, when I observe a growing infant or young people. Young children may appear stupid, doing the wrong things in the eyes of an adult. But that is not what it is, from the kid's perspective. The child simply does not know anything – he is ignorant of the outcome.

The elderly around should guide and must explain the reasons why things are done in a particular way and otherwise. At this very cradle stage I knew I had to do a lot of talking to my kids. At times, the adage, that experience is the best teacher, comes to mind. But the kids must be taught with practical demonstrations.

In some instances, if it's not permanently harmful to the mind and body, one can allow a child to explore his environment while watching him or her. Some of these instances make acquisition of experience faster and indelible. Some societies may frown at the methodology, used to teach a child. It might be labelled as child abuse but discretion should not be disregarded.

Imagine a situation like this.

A friend told me how his young kids used to be fascinated by the flickering flame of a candle, even as they were kept away. They were around 18 months or less in age when he subjected them to the "candle flame" experiment. His wife kept on taking the candle away. It was disturbing to the child and parents. So he suggested that the candle should be left where it was. The child would approach with seductive giggling but on touching the flame, he would scream. There would be hugging till the child stopped crying. And after that experience, which might appear too draconian, the kid never touched a burning candle again. Some parents may never allow their children, learn this way.

It brings to my mind, when my own boisterous younger son, even at his early teenage years, couldn't strike a match. I had to sit him down, that to light a match stick, was not a big deal. That if the burning match stick was held properly, the flame would not burn his fingers. Many sticks were wasted but it took a few years of cajoling before he got rid of that fear. Different strokes, different kids.

Correcting a Child, Through Verbal Communication

Many parents out of frustration and

impatience tend to spank their kids at a tender age. It was not an option for me. I took the hard route of verbal engagement. Although I could shout, which was my own form the dictum of "not - sparing - the - rod".

I simply wanted to influence them by words and actions. I was not enjoying it. Talking was too much for me, my time and my mental energy. I didn't have a choice but my years of sacrifice have given me relief today.

It was a difficult, repetitive but slow route and methodology. The positive results are more permanent and can be seen today. I could recall I told my boys that, the time would come in future, that I would be taking pieces of advice from them. It now happens on a few occasions. I do take their intelligent advice or suggestions of late.
They do disagree with me on a few occasions. I let them be. It's ok and relatively safe.

Ours was a continuous dialogue of over twenty five years. My dialogue became less frequent, as I saw signs that, they had started to mature, in thinking and disposition, after their teenage years. One discovers it was tiring as a father, who is also pursuing a career as a young professional to bring up kids successfully. It is about choice.

Chapter 22: Challenge 5 – Employment Adjustments

Maternity leave only lasts for a certain amount of time. There are also options for paternity leave. Whether one or both parents stay home, you will need to consider that your new responsibility is going to change your employment.

At first, people understand a new parent needs time. After six months or whenever leave expires, the understanding starts to disappear. Employers know that babysitters, family, and other trusted childcare options exist. They do understand that emergencies, such as a cold with high fever will happen. However, missing work because of unnecessary worries will get old and employment can disappear.

If, one parent makes enough to support the entire family, you may decide to have one parent be a stay at home parent. This stay at home parent might also try working from home. There are plenty of telecommuting positions and freelance work due to the internet.

However, it will mean monetary changes. It can also mean that one parent is always with the child, which can bring out resentments. The parent at home can feel smothered. They can feel like they are never without the child, while the other person gets out of the house.

The parent who goes out to work all day may return home tired. This person may expect certain things like the home parent to keep the house clean, do the dishes and laundry, rather than having to help. A downfall is that parents' working from home, making money, do not always have the time to do household chores. They are working and handling a child. It can be tough because work still needs to get done, but the parent has to get up and deal with feeding, diaper changes, arguments between children and all manner of things. Yet, the parent away for the day doesn't remember to think of the challenges.

This parent working out of the house may also think that because they are making more, they should get a break from things at home or be able to have the fun times with the children versus the responsibilities. This same parent may also have a lot of worries about the money coming in or how it is being spent.

The key to these challenges is to find the balance between excessive worry, putting all the child care on one parent, and balancing the budget correctly. In a world where one job does not support a family, adjustments will need to be made to gain proper income for the lifestyle you can live with raising a child or children.

Suggestions for the Employment Challenge

Establish a routine early. When your child is sleeping, you should sleep if you are working from home. When your child is awake, provide toys to keep your child occupied and work. It seems counterintuitive to sleep when your child sleeps because you will have quiet times; however, raising a new child is tiring. If you are trying to be awake when they are asleep, you are missing opportunities to catch up on missed sleep, your work performance will be lower and you will struggle more than if you took a nap.

Seek alternative methods of work. Plenty of telecommuting jobs and freelance jobs exist. Even a little money coming in from a second source is going to help you feel less worried.

Look for part-time employment. It should be something you can do for a few hours a day to bring in money and leave the house. For example, employment based on a favorite hobby, such as working for a small bookstore may suffice.

Sell items online as a living. What are things you haven't used in six months? Can you sell them via eBay or Craigslist?

Perhaps you can post the items on Facebook sales pages?

You have options when it comes to bringing in money. However, you can also point out to the spouse working out of the home that raising your child is a full time job. It is easier to do when both parents are able to experience child care at home.

If you are finding life without a job challenging, then consider child care options. Sometimes friends know of a person with an at home child care business. This type of child care can be less expensive than a mainstream child care location.

Also, don't be afraid to try something. You never know where employment opportunities might present themselves, such as investing in the stock market or real estate. These can be jobs, while providing you flexibility.

When employment worries exist and you are not doing anything to alleviate them, you come to a point of being too emotional and reactive. It can lead to difficulty in your marriage rather than strengthening your marriage now that you share a great bond between you.

Challenges are meant to become your strengths even in parenting. Let your emotions, employment, new responsibilities, lifestyle, and relationship become the elements that make you a stronger person, as well as a dependable spouse. There are numerous rewards that parenting will offer you as long as you can allow these challenges to become your strengths and lead you towards happiness.

Chapter 23: How To Be A Better Step Parent

Not very many of us grow up longing for turning into a step parent, yet individuals are winding up in that role. Being a step mom or step dad can be the most delightful experience, yet it can likewise be devilish. The vast majority would rate it in between; however, nobody can imagine it is generally simple or that there would not be distress, anger, and stupefying times to manage. The most imperative components are time and tolerance: do not expect a lot too early. Growing nearer to the posterity of our loved ones can be superbly compensating with a little practice.

So here are a few tips to help you get that going.

Acknowledge that your partner's kids are permanent: The truth of the matter is whether, you need to be with somebody who has kids, you have to completely acknowledge their posterity is continually going to be a piece of your life.

What kind of individual would your sweetheart be in the event that he or she was cheerful to leave children and girls of a past relationship? These kids have a history with your partner, and irrespective of the extent of love for your partner, their claim is greater. You have to acknowledge this and get accustomed to it. Keep in mind that youngsters have for all intents and purposes nothing to do with whether their folks stay together or not. Every one of this turbulence is unnerving and troublesome for them, especially in light of the fact that they feel that they have no power over what is going on. In this way, they require your thought, admiration and sensitivity.

Try not to be perfect: In case you are excited to be a step parent, you may fall into the trap of attempting to be an extraordinarily decent one. Save your exertion, since this is a Herculean task.

It is ideal to go for essentially being wonderful, intrigued and a decent audience. When step parents first appear on the scene, most kids are suspicious of them. They may think that you have brought on the separation between their folks. They may likewise suspect that you are only a passing phenomenon and in this manner not worth pestering with.

Youngsters can spot somebody who is making a decent attempt a mile away. Try not to give them costly endowments or persist on playing recreations with them before they truly know and feel at peace with you. Simply go about as would be expected and gradually they will acknowledge you.

Give them time with their biological parent: Your partner's kids are continually going to have history and recollections they impart to their biological parent that have nothing to do with you. It is essential to regard that. Along these lines, whatever stage your relationship is at with your partner, dependably bow out of a few activities so that the kids can have their biological parent to themselves some time.

Try not to stress if you cannot love your step kids: If you have offspring of your own, it would be somewhat odd in the event that you felt the same friendship or fondness with your step kids immediately. In time you may turn out to be close, however, do not attempt and drive it. Regardless of the possibility that you have generally needed kids, it is improbable you will feel an instantaneous bond with your partner's children. Numerous step parents will let you know that, as the months and years pass by, you and your step kids can turn out to be exceptionally affectionate to each other, however, this takes time.

Realize that it is characteristic to like some kids superior to others: Individuals do not typically concede if they like any of their own kids more than others. In any case, the truth of the matter is this is really ordinary, regardless of the fact that parents are hesitant to disclose it. This goes twofold for step kids. You may get yourself exceptionally drawn, say, to the most youthful kid who is searching for additional care. Then again you may find that you have a weakness for an especially sensitive kid or a girl who appears to be disregarded in the family in favor of a cleverer or sportier kin.

The truth of the matter is none of us enjoys everyone. It is not a wrong to appreciate one step kid's companionship over another. However, it is indiscreet as well as unkind to demonstrate that partiality. Give all of them presents of equivalent quality at Christmas and birthdays, and spread your consideration however much as could reasonably be expected among every one of the kin. It is essential for both the youngsters, and your association with their biological parent.

We cannot help how we feel, however, we can help what we do about it.

Conclusion

Kids are like arrows in the hand of a warrior. While they stay in your hand, they can be tense and ready to fly. You will be the one to hold them and point their way. Once you release them, all you can do is watch as they fly away from you. Don't let them go too soon, or hold on to them for too long. Take advantage of the time you have with them to direct their feelings, passions and choices. Don't rush their growth by treating them like adults, or treat them like small children forever.

Treat your children with friendship and let them learn what true friendship is all about. Someone who cares, isn't afraid to correct them and show them that they are wrong will gain more respect. Expand and build this relationship through open dialogue, time spent together and dedication to their own interests.

You will always be the map that they will open when they feel lost. Your advice will be the compass for their conscience when the time comes that you are not around. You example will stick with them, even after you die. Your leadership with friendship should be based on mutual respect, trust and loyalty.

Don't expect from them something that you are not also willing to give back. Set rules and standards and enforce them whenever needed, but don't alienate your kids by not explaining why things work best the way that you choose to do them. Your house and family are the fun playground in which they feel safe to grow, make mistakes and heal their wounds.

Remember, there is no such thing as perfection in parenting. We are all trying our best, committed to bringing out the best out in our children, while still trying to do our best in our jobs, with our families and other responsibilities. Your kids will also be your best friends, let them help you, help them and grow together. As a parent, you have much to learn from observation of your kids as they grow up.

www.ingramcontent.com/pod-product-compliance
Lightning Source LLC
Chambersburg PA
CBHW072015070526
44583CB00015B/1486